Aloha B

"Thanks for your support
and Friendship. I shall
always be grateful to
you. Happy Reading"

Wally Amos

1/13/84

Aloha,
"Of all the books
you had to choose
from, thanks for
choosing mine.
Happy Cookie"

Wally Amn
AKA FAMOUS AMOS

THE FAMOUS AMOS STORY

THE
FAMOUS
AMOS
STORY

The Face That Launched a Thousand Chips

WALLY AMOS
with
LEROY ROBINSON

Doubleday & Company, Inc.
Garden City, New York
1983

"It Couldn't Be Done," by Edgar A. Guest, reprinted from *Collected Verse of Edgar A. Guest*, copyright 1934, with permission of Contemporary Books, Inc.

Library of Congress Cataloging in Publication Data

Amos, Wally.
    The Famous Amos story.

    1. Amos, Wally.   2. Businessmen—United States—
Biography.   3. Famous Amos Chocolate Chip Cookie
Corporation.   4. Cookie industry—United States.
I. Robinson, Leroy.   II. Title.
HD9058.C65A46   1983   338.7′6647525 [B]

ISBN: 0-385-19378-5 (hardbound)
ISBN: 0-385-17065-3 (paperback)
Library of Congress Catalog Card Number 80-2842

This book is lovingly dedicated to:

Ruby Amos, my mother, who gave birth to me.

Ruth Wakefield, who gave birth to the chocolate chip cookie.

Aunt Della, who first introduced me to chocolate chip cookies.

Chuck Casell, a dear friend, who helped me give birth to The Famous Amos Chocolate Chip Cookie.

CONTENTS

ACKNOWLEDGMENTS

I have often been referred to as a self-made man. I would like to set the record straight once and for all and also to thank those who actually did help make me what I am today.

First and foremost I acknowledge God as my maker and creator and guide in all I do.

I then would like to thank all my relatives and friends for their contribution in helping me to shape my life. I also must thank the many people who gave so willingly of themselves to help me create The Famous Amos Chocolate Chip Cookie.

I offer a very warm and loving thank you to all of the thousands of people who continue to purchase our cookies. I am also most appreciative to those I meet in my travels who are so generous with their compliments.

Any successful organization is made up of a group of people who care and give their all every day. A great big *brown* thank you to all members of The Famous Amos Family, wherever you may be and in whatever capacity you may perform. I sincerely appreciate your efforts in helping to create and maintain my fame. I could never have done it without you.

Writing a book is no easy task and I had my doubts about finishing. But thanks to my friend Leroy Robinson, my editor, Loretta Barrett, and her assistant, David Gernert, the book was completed. A million thanks to the three of you for helping me tell my story.

A final thank you to my wife, Christine, who loves and supports me in all my projects.

I love you all very much and may God continue to bless you abundantly.

INTRODUCTION

Aloha,

I am an avid reader of inspirational books and a collector of inspirational sayings and messages. I find that I need to do this to reinforce my belief that life is more than I am able to see through my human eyes.

Many years ago I received a Christmas card from a friend, Rene Valente, which contained a message that held a lot of meaning for me. Believing and living that message has given me many happy days. I share it with you in the hope it will do the same for you.

"There is nothing I can give you which you have not; but there is much, very much that, while I cannot give it, you can take. No Heaven can come to us unless our hearts find rest in today. Take Heaven! No peace lies in the future which is not hidden in this present instant. Take Peace!

"The gloom of the world is but a shadow. Behind it, yet within reach, is joy. There is a radiance and glory in the darkness, could we but see, and to see we have only to look. I beseech you to look! Life is so generous a giver, but we, judging its gifts by their covering, cast them away as ugly, or heavy, or hard. Remove the covering and you will find beneath it a living splendor, woven of love, by wisdom, with power.

"Welcome it, grasp it, and you touch the angel's hand that brings it to you. Everything we call a trial, a sorrow, or a duty, believe me, that angel's hand is there. The gift is there, and the wonder of an overshadowing presence. Our joys too; be not content with them as joys. They too conceal diviner gifts.

"And so, at this time, I greet you. Not quite as the world sends greetings, but with profound esteem and with the prayer that, for you, now and forever, the day breaks and the shadows flee away."

Thank you and have a great life.

Wally Amos

 PROLOGUE

"Have a very brown day."

The guests arrived early. Happy feet left their Rollses, VWs, Benzes, and Hondas in the care of young men in red jackets and then stormed the red carpet leading up to the entrance of the shop as though they had found the trail leading to Oz.

Guccis, Nikes, earth shoes, and sandals danced, or moved in some happy manner, into the shop, which was the first stop before joining the festival already under way outside. Inside the shop, the recipients of the 2,500 invitations—many of which had been hand-delivered—signed the guest register and at the same time got a glimpse of the home of the brown and beige fantasy whose birth they had come to celebrate.

Outside, out back, in the tented, AstroTurf parking area, champagne and milk flowed freely. Also the brown and beige fantasies being brought on large cookie sheets at regular intervals were quickly seized by many hands that had waited in anticipation for another opportunity to examine these nutty, chocolate, brown and beige starlets that had created this overflow of worshipers. And space, like the precious morsels on the cookie sheets, was at a premium. But that didn't matter to the happy celebrants, all of whom were in sync with either the rhythm of their excited hearts, or the West Indian Steel Drum Band, or the roving Dixieland Jazz Ensemble, or the movement of the dancers. This carnival of dancers had contracted *brown fever*, which was evident by the way they danced to whatever while carrying their drinks in one hand, their souvenir balloons and posters in another hand, and kept their mouths filled with the brown and beige morsels while happily chanting, "Have a very brown day."

This was all happening on Sunday, March 9, 1975, in Los Angeles, where I had invited all of my friends, and their friends, to the first home of The Famous Amos Chocolate Chip Cookie. The corner of Sunset Boulevard and Formosa Avenue, the location of our home, was jammed with people coming and going—new friends and old friends of mine, and now Friends of The Cookie. Traffic on Sunset was stop and go, slow and curious, and finally stopped, with cars parking wherever so as to get a taste of this fun in the sun and also to "have a very brown day."

For a while it seemed as though I might have to settle for a rainy day to celebrate this opening day. After all, the previous week had been rain and nothing but rain, with no sign of letting up. Then, on the morning of my planned celebration, the sky was overcast and gray, but not my faith. I told myself that I just knew that God had not let me get *this* close to fulfilling my dream of the last four months so as to rain on my parade.

And I was right, because not only did the sky go from a sad-faced gray to a cheery and bright blue, when those gray cloud doors opened up the warm rays of the sun gave me my own summer day in early spring. Also, all of the invited guests of The Cookie arrived bearing their own sunshine of happiness and good cheer. But what was most evident was their serious case of brown fever, which I had been spreading the last four months. And this was confirmed when they would say, "Have a very brown day," just before they disappeared inside with the other fevered frolickers.

The brown fever had touched everyone from every walk of life. Even the mayor of the city of Los Angeles, Thomas Bradley, who could not be there, sent greetings and word that March 9, 1975, was, in fact, "The Famous Amos Chocolate Chip Cookie Day" in Los Angeles. And with that piece of news I was touched—to tears and nostalgia.

I thought of what I had been doing before I went on what

I called the Cookie Trip; I thought of B. J. Gilmore, and how she had planted the seed that became the idea which brought about this day; I thought of the supporters, the investors, and the nonsupporters and disbelievers, some of whom were present today at this opening-day celebration and saying to each other, "Who would've thought all of this would happen because of a chocolate chip cookie?"

"I did!" I said to myself when I heard them. I believed, because I made the commitment. But I knew at this moment I was not alone. I had God. And the universe, because I believe God *is* the universe, and not some guy who punishes you when you're evil or bad, or rewards you if you're good and kind. It's an energy, or force, within the universe which we all feel so often in our lifetimes. But too many times we fail to realize that what we're feeling is actually the power of God. And it's that power which turns us this way and that way, daily, and in a direction that is always for our highest good. That's what was with me when I made the commitment. And that's when I went to work designing my future, as well as working as hard as I had to to make it happen: I had the will of the universe.

Also, at this moment, I recalled something that was said to me a long time ago by Oscar Brown, Jr., one of my show business clients. When he said it I knew it was something special. But it wasn't until this special day of my life that I was able to understand the full meaning of Oscar's words, and just how meaningful they were to me and what had happened to me.

"Life is rhythm," Oscar had said to me. "There's a certain rhythm to life. And if you can be in step with that rhythm, then your life flows."

That was what had happened; that was what was happening this March day in 1975 when Wally Amos also became known as Famous Amos. That was why everyone was happily applauding their approval. That was why I could look out in the crowd and see many old friends; former show business clients; my mother Ruby; my sons Michael, Gregory, and Shawn; my best friend Chuck Fly; and so many other people who had played a role, large and small, in my life prior to this day. They were all present giving their approval and acknowledging the fact that I had *finally* gotten in step with the rhythm of life. And they also knew how long, and how much, it had taken for me to reach this day.

*I believe that if I try my best, and we do
our best, we shall be the best.*

At 1 A.M. on July 1, 1936, my scream signaled the rhythm of
life in the only son born to Wallace and Ruby Amos, and in
the tiny two-room house, located about twenty-five yards from
the railroad tracks in the black section of Tallahassee, Florida,
happiness and prayers prevailed. But so did the fact that I was
born on the heels of the Great Depression, and that meant
Ruby could not spend too much time at home recuperating, or
enjoying her new son, Wallace, Jr. These were hard times, and
for Ruby and Wallace, who could not read or write, keeping
their jobs came first.

Having both parents working did not deprive me of the
southern breeding that comes with being southern born. No
matter what the conditions were in the outside world—meaning the world outside of the South—my life was one of strict
religious instruction and good manners. And because both
Wallace and Ruby were serious about religion, they kept my
training in that area continuous. This meant there would be
very few fun days, as some people know them. Anything that
appeared to be fun, like dancing, was a sin in the Amos home.
Anything that was not part of the tenets of the strict religious
diet I was being fed I had better not do. Therefore dancing was
something I did not learn to do during those youthful years in
Tallahassee. However, there were other things I had to learn,
and make sure I practiced, or I would pay a high price.

Early in my youth I learned all about both of my parents: Wallace had more bark than bite, and Ruby barked the loudest, plus she had the biggest bite. She was the chief disciplinarian. All of this disciplining had nothing to do with my being terribly mischievous as a boy. It was just that Ruby was always firm in her instructions to me—or anyone for that matter. And if her instructions were not followed to the letter, then you might as well be prepared to deal with something you hadn't bargained for. But, despite my advance knowledge of what could happen if I crossed Ruby, I seemed to make the mistake of challenging her from time to time. And that was not too smart of me, because I would never end up the winner, just the recipient of a sore behind.

Winning, I'm certain now, was not what I needed at that time of my youth. The fact is, had I won it might surely have contributed to my being a loser sometime in the future when I became an adult. So Ruby's disciplining me was for my own good. I don't think I would be the person I am today if she had not been so strict and so committed to her reasons for disciplining me. I'm also certain that my daily adherence to Ruby's commands was responsible for my discovery that there is more than a little of Ruby Amos in me. And definitely a lot more than of my father, Wallace, whom I was named after, but whom I had little in common with.

But, when you really get down to it, it's not the name but what is inside a person that matters most. My father was to me and those who knew him a good person, for a number of reasons. The most apparent was his willingness to always remain true to himself and to his station in life. He had no education to speak of, but he was a hardworking man. He was a laborer at the local gas plant, a job he remained in for his entire working life. Wallace was not aggressive like Ruby, and he never made an effort to challenge her position of chief disciplinarian. This, of course, did not mean that Wallace was not capable of severe damage if necessary, because he was. And during one of the rare times I was given a "beating" by Wallace for something I had done wrong, I thought the end had come for sure.

The moment is memorable because it provided me a

clearer insight into just what kind of person my father was. For instance, the "beating" I received was more a psychological one for me, while it was merely a symbolic one for Wallace. However, you could not have explained that to me at the time he pulled his belt from his waist with rage in his eyes and face. Nor would you have been able to convince me that his raised hand holding the belt was not going to be the end of me once his belt made contact with my body. And, of course, leading up to that fateful moment I was yelling and raising my wail an octave each time it appeared he would strike me. Finally, when Wallace did strike me, I hardly felt the blow. It was almost laughable—which I didn't do—this "beating" I was receiving from Wallace. Suddenly it became apparent to me that the louder I wailed the lighter the blow would be. Therefore I performed better than a newborn baby who's just been slapped on its soft behind.

After the so-called "beating" I just knew that I had put one over on Wallace, and I felt proud of myself. However, as memory serves me, Ruby was in the adjoining room, and Wallace knew that Ruby strongly believed in the beating as a direct form of discipline. Therefore, Wallace had actually put one over on me and Ruby. And thinking about it now, I'm certain that beatings were just not Wallace's way of life.

And just like beatings, father and son moments were quite limited between Wallace and me. But when we did get to spend time together it was always special for me. No matter what it was—visiting him at the plant and using his Lava soap to take a shower (and almost losing my skin as well), or having him take me for my monthly Saturday haircut—I treasured those moments of being alone with my father. But those moments, like Wallace Amos, were rare. Too rare. But I've learned to love and accept "Mr. Wallace," as he was affectionately called by the kids in the neighborhood, for what he was: a man doing the best he knew how to do with what he had to work with. And, although I was not heavily influenced by him, I know that I did pick up that latter trait: doing the best I can with what I have to work with.

Ruby didn't have any more to work with than Wallace, but she was something else altogether. And I say that with a great deal of affection for this industrious lady who is my mother, but whom I lovingly call Ruby. As a child, however, I dared not call her by her first name, nor did I have the high regard I eventually developed for her. But that's only because a child has a very limited perspective of why parents are the way they are. When you grow older certain things become quite apparent, in this case Ruby's commitment and consistency. She was always full of life, and willing to take on all of life's challenges, and never complained once.

It was almost as though Ruby had decided at an early age that she would have to work hard all of her life, and if that was the way it was going to be, then she was going to be the best and hardest worker there was. Well, without being able to read or write, the only work for a black woman in the South who did not live on a farm was as a domestic. So that meant Ruby helped support the family by washing someone else's windows, floors, clothes, and children. And it didn't matter what Ruby was called upon to do, she would do it with fervor and professionalism. For that reason alone, Ruby was one of the most in-demand domestics working in Tallahassee—a fact that made her one of the highest paid in her field, and the busiest. It also meant she was absent from her own home for most of the days during the week, something that didn't bother me or Wallace, who also seemed to be spending a lot of time away from home, even when Ruby was not working. Had I been aware of such things, I would have realized that the reason for Wallace's and Ruby's absenteeism was that they were becoming incompatible day by day. However, I was too young to know about that word, and Ruby and Wallace wouldn't have known what it meant had they heard it.

But, despite the absence of both parents from my home, I was not an abandoned child. Ruby realized that, and our neighbors made sure of it. One thing about southern living, your neighbors are all just like family. And since our community was only twenty families, I had twenty replacements for Wallace and Ruby, and twenty reminders that Ruby's commandments should not be broken. You see, another important part of southern breeding is always practicing good manners and exercising respect for your elders, something that was taken for granted and practiced daily. However, for an energetic young man like me, being courteous sometimes got in the way of the games my friends and I would be playing. It was like having a job, the only difference being that I was not paid for minding my manners, only if I forgot to.

No matter what time of day it was or what I was doing at the time, if I saw someone older than I entering or leaving a home in the community, I had better speak. "Yes, ma'am," "No, sir," "Hello, ma'am," "Good-bye, sir," and "Thank you, ma'am" were the allowed responses. And if you saw the same person coming in and out of the house three or four times within a twenty-minute period, their presence had to be acknowledged. Some days it took more than nine innings to get through a game of baseball. But this was the law of the southern land I grew up in, and of Ruby in particular. And there was no breaking that law, even in Ruby's absence, because she always found out. Believe me, I soon became very willing to give up my chance at bat; it was a lot better than going home and being hit by Ruby.

Being courteous wasn't always fun for me as a boy, but it certainly turned out to be rewarding during my adult life, both personally and professionally. It was Ruby's Friday night fish fries which first showed me how good manners could contribute to good business.

In just about every black community in the South, Friday night was, traditionally, set aside for fish fries, as they were called. Actually, fish wasn't the only food available. There would be plenty of fried chicken, potato salad, collard greens, black-eyed peas and rice (hoppin' John), corn bread and hot rolls, as well as various cakes and sweet potato pie, which was all washed down with red soda water. It was a soul food feast, which everyone was ready and able to partake of because Friday was also the day "the eagle flew"—payday in black Ameri-

can colloquialism. And when Ruby got to work frying up fish
and chicken, letting the satisfying aroma of these rich foods
run rampant throughout the community, everybody ran to
Ruby's Friday night fish fry.

The fish fries were also good for socializing. Most of the
people who came to buy also came to socialize with their
friends whom they would not see the entire week. And for
those who did not want to come out, there were deliveries,
which was where I came in. I didn't mind the work; I got to
eat my share of fish "samiches," and all the other goodies as
well.* For me, this was my favorite time of the week, the Friday night fish fry, and I looked forward to this day in much
the same way I looked forward to Christmas in December.
The other young bachelors, however, looked forward to Saturday night, because that was when they would "do the Devil's
work," according to the more religious townpeople. What
that meant was, these young men would go out drinking
and "chasing women." But, come Sunday, all of those same
young men would be finished with the "Devil's work" and
would show up in church Sunday morning to learn the Lord's
lessons. It seemed as though going to church on Sunday, and
letting the preacher see them there, was their penance for the
last twenty-four hours. But this penance only lasted until the
next Saturday.

I did not get in on doing any of the "Devil's work," naturally, because I was too young, but I did attend church every
Sunday. I was there because Wallace and Ruby insisted upon
it, and not because my soul needed cleansing. As I got older
and into my early teens, I did have reason for penance because
of my thoughts about girls, which I dared not let Ruby find out
about. However, as far as Ruby and Wallace were concerned,
they were seeing that I got a good Christian education because
it had been ordained early in my youth that my "calling" was to
the pulpit.

There are a number of reasons why it was believed that I
would one day become a preacher. First of all, the fact that I

* This was also where my manners, thanks to Ruby, came in: I made
great tips.

not only attended church every Sunday, I went to the Wednesday night prayer meetings (a tradition of the black Church) with either Ruby or Wallace. And by the time I was eight years old I had learned all the books of the Bible, including the Old and New Testaments. Reciting those books was my specialty on those Sundays we would visit churches with such a program. I was even baptized at an early age—which was actually called "getting religion." The truth is, I never really did. I could never bring myself to *see* or *feel* what the older members of the Church experienced. And when I did go forth for baptism it was not so much that I had gotten religion, it simply had gotten me. The best I can recall of my decision to go forth was because I didn't want to continue week after week not getting religion, so I got it too. However, with all that was predicted, I never got a "calling" that I could hear to become a preacherman.

Just as important as my religious education was the more formal education of reading, writing, and arithmetic. Many of the black parents in the South did not have the opportunity of going to school, so for their children it was a *must*, even if it meant going to segregated schools. But the truth of the matter was, a segregated education was the only thing available to blacks in the South during my youth. There was also only one school, a combination elementary-high school which was approximately four miles from where I lived. And because there were no school buses for the black school, we all had to walk. On bad-weather days I would get to ride the city bus. But, even with these inconveniences, you went to school every day, and you had better not forget what you learned at home, such as your good manners.

Our teachers were just as demanding as our parents, and did not tolerate insolence of any kind. Anyone who decided to challenge this—and there were very few challengers—would be entitled to either a paddling on the behind or a whack across the palm of the hands with a ruler. And on top of this painful experience was the note that would go home with you, which was an instant licking. Ruby didn't tolerate bad manners or disrespect to *anyone*, even if the segregation laws permitted it.

Ruby was the kind of person who didn't buy too many things that she did not start. Segregation was not something she had started and, given the right reason, she was not above changing the law of the land, which she came close to doing one Sunday when she and I were returning home from church.

The law of the land at the time was that black people sat in the back of the bus, while white people sat in the front. This particular day Ruby decided to sit in the front of the bus since it was practically empty, except for a young white woman who was the bus driver's girlfriend. It was next to this white woman that Ruby decided to take her seat. And Ruby felt justified in her decision, because we had done a lot of walking that day and her feet were hurting. Almost immediately the white woman complained to the bus driver, who turned to Ruby and *told* her to move to the rear of the bus. The problem with this was that Ruby usually did the telling.

"I paid my money and I'm gonna sit where I please," was Ruby's militant response to the driver. This was not acceptable, and I anticipated trouble. And, sure enough, as soon as the bus had reached one of the depots on the route, the driver went inside to get some direction or help in handling Ruby, an "uppity nigger." The driver returned suddenly, and alone. This being Sunday, which was usually calm, peaceful, and without "uppity niggers," especially since this was 1944, there was no help for the driver. So the driver *told* Ruby once again to move to the rear of the bus. And once again Ruby stoutly refused.

There was a standoff, at least long enough for the driver to figure out what he should do next: physically move Ruby to where he demanded she go, or move on about his business of driving the bus. The driver, after examining who else was on the bus, decided to concede this moment and return to his bus route. His decision was a wise one since the other passengers were all black young men wearing the uniform of the U.S. Army, and they were sitting quietly waiting for the driver's next move.

During this incident I sat quiet and a bit frightened. Not so much for what the driver might have done to Ruby, or what the black soldiers might have done to protect Ruby, but be-

cause whenever Ruby raised her voice I became frightened for
anyone who defied my mother. But, more important, I saw my
mother display a courage I was proud of. And then, ten years
later when Rosa Parks refused to give up her seat to a white
passenger in Montgomery, Alabama, and triggered the well-
known bus boycott led by Dr. Martin Luther King, Jr., I recalled Ruby's courage. I thought, at that moment, had things
gone another way that day in Tallahassee on that bus, Ruby
would have been the first *famous* Amos.

The first four years of my formal and southern education
were spent at Lincoln Elementary-High School, and I don't
have many memories of that period of my life. I do remember
getting my first taste of show business when I won a talent
contest for my singing. I won first prize, but my plans did not
include becoming a child prodigy, at least as far as Ruby and
Wallace were concerned. My education at Lincoln was ade-
quate at best, and for some parents not good enough, especially
the parents at Ruby's church. They wanted a little more than
what the segregated city schools were offering and decided to
do something about it. That something was an elementary
school which was started at Ruby's church, near our home,
where I went after completing my first four years of schooling
at Lincoln.

Although the school was a part of the church, it was not
bound by parochial rules. It was, however, the first school of its
kind in Tallahassee, and it was unique in other ways. The fact
that the classes were smaller than the ones at Lincoln meant
there were greater opportunities to learn. At the public school
we had to almost fight for an education, although there was an
abundance of extracurricular activities to participate in, many
of which brought attention upon me. But what I needed—attention as a student—I never received at Lincoln.

That was definitely not the situation at the church school,
nor the intentions of our only two dedicated teachers, Mrs.
Moore and Mrs. Woodbury. They were committed to our
young minds, and to opening them up to a world we would one

day be doing things for, doing things in, and changing. In other words, we were made to *think*, to be curious about *why* things were the way they were, to seek solutions, but not to add to the problems.

For a ten-year-old that was probably quite a bit to understand. But it was not so much understanding as *seeing what is possible* with an education, curiosity, and commitment. In other words, we were being provided the tools that would at some point bring us in touch with the "rhythm of life," a reality I would one day live.

Due to the tight reins Ruby always kept on me, most of my curiosity was directed more to the things which she said I couldn't do, and which were basically taboo in our house. And certainly girls were among those prohibited areas, which amplified my curiosity, especially when one of the girls in my neighborhood would make dates with me because she wanted me to wrestle with her. I was never sure about her motives, but that didn't matter. What mattered was how good her body felt next to mine when we would wrestle. And my curiosity wouldn't let me stop.

Another event brought me in contact with some older girls who would always tell me how cute I was. It was difficult—even at my young age—not to be flattered by such comments. However, when they said they would wait for me until I got older, I was totally confused about what they meant. Why, or how old, I didn't know. But when I reached that age of curiosity, I went looking for these older girls to see about that promise. They were no longer around, which left me a little disappointed. I was not sure if it was because they didn't keep their promise, or how naive I was when it was made.

But those experiences, plus many others, taught me a thing or two. Because when I finally met Kitty, my special girlfriend, I made sure I didn't listen to any promises which couldn't be kept right away. And by then Kitty and I had a standing date to meet Saturdays at the movies—the major entertainment for blacks in Tallahassee at the time. Those meetings were a high point in my life because I was experiencing puppy love. And the dark theater was perfect for Kitty and me to carry on our torrid romance. Soon, however, this began to lose interest for me as I realized how much more I could enjoy if I had the money. So that was when I decided to use my Saturdays making money instead of making love, and I put together my very first business venture.

Actually, I made the shoeshine box which helped me to get my business going. But it was the locations and my own hustling which made the shoeshine business a success. And my reputation of giving great shoeshines became known throughout our community. Naturally a lot of Ruby had rubbed off on me, which was certainly evident in my decision to extend my profits by taking on more work. That's when I decided to deliver the local newspaper, the Tallahassee *Democrat*, which did increase my weekly income, but it was rough on my feet.

However, my hard work and pain did not go unnoticed by Wallace and Ruby, who must have been sympathetic as well as proud of my accomplishments. Because one day they surprised me with my first set of wheels—a beautiful red two-wheeler bicycle, which I didn't know how to ride. But I was committed to my newspaper route, so I learned to ride that bicycle in no time, and I became one of the best newspaper boys for the Tallahassee *Democrat*.

With all that I was doing—girls, school, and my business enterprises—there was little time for having a lot of male friends. Of the few I did have, Ralph Robinson, Jr., is the most memorable. Although Ralph was three years younger than I there was something special about him. And thinking back, there is one very vivid moment I recall now that explains best why Ralph was so important to me as a friend. It was during one of our winter months when in other parts of the world snow was a regular happening. But in Tallahassee, Florida, all you could do was wish for snow, and that's exactly what Ralph and I did. I remember we sat at the window wishing very hard for snow. And our wishes were so strong we actually began to see snowflakes falling from the sky. The fact that neither of us had ever seen snow did not stop us from wishing for something that was better than what we had thus far been exposed to.

That memorable day is indicative to me that Ralph was

my friend because he, like me, was looking for the best in a situation that seemed hopeless. And twenty-nine years later when I spoke to Ralph again in Detroit, where he lives and works, he was still looking for the best in bad situations. At the time he was a paramedic whose daily work was trying to save lives: seeing hope for life when life is thought to be hopeless. Finding his vision had not changed, I was proud he was my friend.

I also appreciated the fact that most of the adults I came in contact with would never let me be exposed to anything but the best in them, like "Mr. Bootsy," who was one of my favorite people in Tallahassee. It was with Mr. Bootsy—whose real name was Julius Fisher—and his wife, whom we called Miss Annie, that I spent a lot of time, since they lived so close to us. Many a day I would watch him do various things, ask him and Miss Annie many questions going through my mind, and enjoy all the good that was available for me to see in both of them with my youthful eyes. But the first person to *really* open my eyes to seeing the good in people was my Granny, Annie Hawkins.

Granny was Wallace's mother, and she had remarried after Wallace's father died. She married a man I remember as someone I called "Man," although I don't remember why. His actual name was Harry Hawkins, but he was Man to me. But Granny was the one I remembered best. And why not! She was the first person who ever spoiled me, and she saved me from Ruby more than a few times. Granny also showed me a very tender and understanding kind of love. Early in my developing life I lost that love and Granny, and the good I would *always* see in her, which was her legacy to me. It has, therefore, been my daily desire to try and find something good in everyone I meet.

My childhood in Tallahassee was like kids everywhere: living life to the fullest every day, going to bed every night tired and happy, and looking forward to the next day's experiences with great anticipation. Then one morning during the summer of 1948 I awakened to a day I had not anticipated. It was the day I found out that I would be moving to Orlando, Florida, to live with Ruby's mother, but that Wallace would not be going with us. The marriage of Ruby and Wallace was over.

Actually it had been over long before this decision to separate. Prior to their decision the occasional arguments became more constant, and bitter fights ensued. But even before that they seldom did anything together, nor did the three of us do anything as a family. Wallace had his friends and Ruby had hers. They didn't even practice religion together; Wallace was Baptist, Ruby was Methodist, and my religious instructions were received at both churches.

There were very few times that I can remember when they showed any warmth and affection for each other or, worst of all, to me. They were two serious people, and laughter was seldom heard in our home. That's probably why I enjoy laughing so much and have become such a great audience for anything that smacks of humor. But not Ruby and Wallace. I guess some of the reason for their not taking the time to laugh more was because they were too busy trying to make a living and bring me up right. And during that struggle they lost sight of the love that must have brought them together; the love that went into producing me, and the love that might have kept our family together.

Whatever it could have been was not possible now that they had made their decision to separate. My life was now going to be different. I was leaving Tallahassee, and our family would now consist of Ruby and me, with Wallace as someone I would visit from time to time.

2

Success does not come to you. You go to it.

Actually, there was a three-way separation of the Amos family: Wallace remained in Tallahassee, Ruby moved to Orlando with me, and a month later I moved to New York without Ruby.

It was an idea that appealed to me; not the separation from both my parents, but moving to the "Big Apple," New York City. I had visited there the summers of 1946 and 1947, and for this southern-born, southern-bred, scared-to-death, skinny black kid it was a breathtaking experience, especially the tall buildings. The tallest building I had ever seen was five stories, and there were very few of those in Tallahassee. New York's concrete jungle is as intimidating as it is awesome. It's as though the Empire State Building and all the rest are looking down at you with the warning: "Rise above all of this, or get out of the way!"

But despite the intimidating ambience of New York, thousands of people travel there either as tourists or as immigrants. And hundreds of thousands live their entire lives trying to find out if there is any truth to the belief that "if you can make it in New York, you can make it anywhere." That may have been on the minds of Ruby and her mother, Julia, when they told me how great the "opportunities for blacks" were, which was also their way of encouraging me not to fret for having to make the trip by myself. If they had listened to my heartbeat they would have realized how excited this twelve-year-old was just at the idea of the train ride that would carry me to my new home. And the fact that I would be making the trip alone was the best part of all: I felt as if I had reached my manhood.

Riding the Silver Meteor, the classy, sleek-looking, bullet-like train of the Pennsylvania Railroad, was the greatest excitement to my young mind. This being 1948, it was a uniquely fast train, making the trip to Pennsylvania Station in twenty-four hours. For blacks traveling on the Silver Meteor, the opportunity to sit in the large roomy seats of the coaches almost compensated for the fact that segregated seating was a must while traveling in the South. However, once the train was out of the South integration went into effect.

When I said good-bye to Ruby and Grandma Julia in Orlando, I don't know if I was more excited about the train trip or the shoebox full of food Ruby had prepared for me. In those days—and probably these days as well—blacks traveling on any of the public conveyances would always bring their meals with them. This was another must when traveling in the South because of the segregation laws. In all the depots food was off limits to blacks, and many times the drinking fountain and restrooms were too. Therefore, it became traditional among black travelers to carry enough rations to get them to their destination. So the shoebox became the lunch pail, so to speak, and for me and most every black person it was a real treat. What Ruby, and other black mothers, could do with an ordinary shoebox was incredible. Thinking about it now, had the shoe manufacturers realized what was going on, they would have charged extra for the box when selling shoes to black people in the South.

For instance, my shoebox meal was fit for a king—well, a twelve-year-old king. It consisted of fried chicken—the drumstick, which was my favorite, and another old wives' tale that contributed to my so-called "calling" to the pulpit—if you liked the drumstick of the chicken you were going to be a preacher—boiled eggs, rich yellow pound cake, cheese, and some fruit. Simple. Tasty. And this would be my breakfast, lunch, and dinner until I reached my destination. About the only thing missing was something to drink, which I had money to purchase from the vendor on the train. That was another great opportunity I felt happy about, being able to decide on and purchase my own drink. Big deal? Yes, it was.

Not too long after I had left Orlando I attacked my shoebox of food. It was just as well that I ate as soon as I did because the hum of the train had a hypnotic effect, and I fell asleep as soon as it got dark. I also slept the entire night, and just about the entire trip. When I did wake up it was because the train jerked as it was leaving its most recent stop. It was the morning of the next day, and we were inching closer and closer to New York City. All of a sudden I began to feel an excitement that I had never known; I also began to have small fears as to how I would make the adjustment. Two short summer visits were one thing, but living in New York permanently was a reality that was just beginning to hit me. But I couldn't turn back now. So I let my thoughts race with the train into Pennsylvania Station and the beginning of my new life.

When I stepped off the train at Penn Station, my little body was quickly pulled into the emotional and happy arms of Aunt Della, whom I would be living with, and Aunt Lillie. They were both so excited about my arrival that I felt like a hero of sorts. But I immediately became confused when they started laughing at me, which was partially explained when Aunt Della said: "Boy, you're a sight for sore eyes."

And I guess I was. I had gotten off the train carrying the now messy shoebox of leftover food in one hand and my shoeshine box in the other. It was the shoeshine box which drew the laughter and got me the kind of look from my two aunts, who were now sophisticated New Yorkers, for someone who looks "country." For me it was quite natural to carry my shoeshine box. After all, Ruby had always made it a point to me that I should keep my shoes shined, and moving to New York was no reason to stop. Also, my shoeshine box had provided my first opportunity to be in business and to make money, something I had developed an obsession for. Therefore, it had been my intention to make some money with my shoeshine box on the train, no matter how it looked. However, I was so excited about the trip, I completely forgot why I had brought the shoeshine box along. The reaction to the shoeshine box made me remember, but by then it was a source of embarrassment instead of making money. If I've learned anything since that incident, it is that no matter what others think you should be, or how you should look, it matters only that *you* are happy with who you are. As the title of Rev. Terry Cole-Whitaker's book suggests, "What You Think of Me Is None of My Business."

Once the laughing died down, we were on our way to Aunt Della's home, which we traveled to by subway. This, too, was a great source of fascination, the 245 route miles the subway spans, taking in just about the entire breadth of the five boroughs which comprise New York City. And the subway we took was the A train. However, unlike Duke Ellington's classic song, "Take the 'A' Train," we were not going to Harlem. Aunt Della lived in an area called Washington Heights, so named because George Washington once had his headquarters in the area. Now it consisted of many brownstone buildings, one of which Aunt Della lived in with her husband Fred Bryant, and Joe, Uncle Fred's son by a previous marriage. When our subway train arrived at the Amsterdam Avenue and 163rd Street station, we had only a short walk to my new home, which was at 567 West 161st Street. That walk, however, was not without some anxiety.

I was still feeling embarrassed by the greeting I had received at Penn Station because I was carrying my shoeshine box, which I still had with me. Therefore, I was uneasy about seeing anyone I might know. And as it always turns out, the confrontations you don't want to have are the ones which invariably take place. So the first person I met when I came out of the subway was Walter Carter, a friend my age I had met during my summer visits, and someone who would eventually become my best friend once my roots were firmly planted in New York City.

After surviving Walter's unusual glance and nod, which I returned, we arrived at Aunt Della's one-bedroom apartment, which was all of about 1,000 square feet, and nowhere near enough room for three. And now I would make four in the second-floor apartment, which was not easy to get around in. Aunt Della and Uncle Fred had the only bedroom, and I shared my cousin Joe's bedroom, which was actually the living room during the day. Becoming Joe's roommate, so to speak, I got my first experience in what it's like having a bedroom which is also the apartment's entrance. But, more important, I was exposed to what *giving*, in the truest sense of the word, was all about by Aunt Della and Uncle Fred letting me share their tiny home. But it was my home now, whether I felt guilty or not, until Ruby saved up enough money to join me.

Aunt Della became Ruby's replacement, but she was 180 degrees out of phase with her sister. Unlike Ruby, Aunt Della was happy and jovial all the time. She was also forever battling to lose weight, which was not easy because she loved to eat and to cook. My Aunt Della also had a tremendous sense of humor and was a great one for practical jokes—with me a regular customer. But being the butt of her jokes was not without educational value. Once she revealed to me my obsession for money by offering to pay me if I would kiss her feet. After a brief deliberation with myself, I rationalized, "What the heck. They're clean feet," and made some "easy money," I felt. That really made me see I'd do *anything* for money, and how wrong that was.

Not too long after my arrival in New York, I was really taught a lesson. One day when I was on my way to buy a pair of sneakers at a sporting goods store in Harlem, I was approached by a boy in his late teens who wanted me to do him a favor. It seemed he wanted me to pick up some money owed to him at an apartment which he would take me to. I told him where I was going, but he assured me it would not take any time. And, besides, he would pay me for doing it. Considering the offer, and the fact that it was "easy money," I told the teenager I would do it. I was so proud of myself, and I couldn't wait to get back home to tell Aunt Della about the "easy money" I had made.

When I arrived with the teenager at the building where I was to pick up the money, I should have asked myself why he didn't pick it up himself, but I didn't. Instead, I went into the building, with the teenager following me, and continued to the top floor, which was abandoned, and there I faced the moment of truth. I turned to the teenager and a knife he was holding, pointed at my face. He then stripped me of the money I had to buy my sneakers, an identification bracelet, and a silver Mickey Mouse ring. The ring had been purchased in Tallahassee with my own money, and if I still had it today it would be a collector's item. But it's gone because I allowed myself to be *had*, just to find out that there was no such thing as "easy money."

Aunt Della picked me up at the police station, where I had gone scared, crying, and ashamed of my stupidity. And Aunt Della and the rest of the family did not let me forget what my greed for money had gotten me. They teased me for a long time after that.

In addition to teaching me to use good sense in my judgment of people and in my obsession for money, Aunt Della reunited me with her delicious homemade chocolate chip cookies. I had first experienced these cookies, which were like no other cookies I had ever tasted before, on a summer visit. I was ten years old at the time, and the experience was one I always cherished. Ruby, who always baked delicious cakes and pies for her fish fries in Tallahassee, had never baked cookies, particularly chocolate chip cookies like Aunt Della's. And because I couldn't have Aunt Della's chocolate chip cookies, I would never eat any others being sold in the stores in Tallahassee. It was as if my taste buds refused any other chocolate chip cookies if they did not have the original taste of Aunt Della's. Therefore, when I wasn't off learning how to operate on the mean streets of New York City, I had the pleasure of licking Aunt Della's mixing bowl when she made her chocolate chip cookies. And by being further exposed to her tasty recipe, although I didn't know it then, I was committing to my taste buds' memory my future, although I still had a lot of growing to do first.

Despite the number of experiences I had been through that summer in New York, when September rolled around I was still timid, shy, and full of apprehension. I was still, in part, a "country boy." But the fear of the unknown—such as going to a new school—was still with me, and I didn't look forward to that first day in school, which also meant meeting new boys and girls and hoping they would accept me.

Actually, I was more concerned with what class I would be put into at Edwin W. Stitt Junior High School. Usually, students coming from the South were "put back" because southern educations were supposedly inferior to the education provided in northern schools. Well, that move by Ruby and the other mothers to establish the church school paid off, because I was placed in my correct grade, and by the way I handled the work, my southern education had been better than most. However, I had one other obstacle to overcome: getting used to the idea of attending an integrated school.

Public School 164, which was the alternate identity of my school, typical of most elementary and junior high schools in the New York public school system, was a mini-United Nations. And my class was truly an integrated one, with Chinese, Puerto Ricans, Jews, Italians, Irish, and blacks. But when I met Eddie Gang, who was Chinese, I was taken aback. It wasn't that I had not known there were Chinese people, I just had never been this close to one, or any Asian person, because they didn't exist, as far as I was concerned, in Tallahassee.

Ignazio Mendez, who was Puerto Rican, was less foreign to me, but I was still surprised to hear he spoke English so well. And Gary Ecker, who was Jewish, was the first white student I had ever attended school with, or had any dealings with at all. I soon realized that Gary, Ignazio, Eddie Gang, and many of the black students were all the same: they all had their own personalities, whatever their color, and if I liked or disliked them it was probably for that reason. As for the girls in my class, if they were pretty I tried to be their friends no matter what their personalities were.

This "liberal" attitude about girls was not because I was girl crazy or anything like that. I was a shy person at first and found it hard to express myself. That was one of the reasons Hazel Weston, a beautiful light-brown black girl who I developed an immediate crush on, never noticed me. It was the same thing with Jean Parker, an ebony goddess who had the best shape of all the girls in our class. I thought I'd *never* get to know the girls.

Eventually, however, I gained confidence—I was a bit of a show-off—and my attempts to make friends in school met with success. Outside the school, I met the unfriendly members of gangs, which were prevalent in New York but unheard of in Tallahassee. And none of my friends in school had told me about gangs or what to expect. My previous encounter with the teenage con artist kind of prepared me, but when a muscular, tough-looking boy came up to me and asked that I "loan" him a nickel, I was thrown off. And I thought to myself, "I don't even know him, so why should I loan him anything?" Besides, at the time I only had a quarter, and I wasn't gonna give that up. So, appearing to be brave, but really frightened, I said: "I ain't got no money."

"All I find, I have?" was the reply of the tough boy, the common expression used when making a "shakedown." It was also a warning that if he searched me and found I had been lying I would be out of money and maybe some teeth. Considering the possibilities, I chose to part with my money and keep my teeth, which were still the original ones I was born with.

This time, to avoid the humiliation, I didn't tell Aunt Della what had happened. But avoiding this tough boy was something I would have to do, or end up broke all the time. As it turned out, I didn't have to do anything. It was soon learned by the tough boy and his gang members that Joe was my cousin. And because Joe was as big and as old as the largest gang member, the word was put out in the neighborhood to keep "hands off" of me. In fact the tough boy became my friend, although he didn't return my quarter. But he didn't take any more of my money, nor did any other gang members, either.

Eventually it became clear that if this skinny, timid kid was going to survive other gangs I would have to become a more self-assured skinny kid. That meant I would have to join a gang, or start my own, which I did. We called ourselves the

Marquis, but we were not like the tough boys gang. We were actually a social club, and our goal was to *make* money, not *take* it from timid kids like me.

Joining me in the Marquis were my best friend, Walter Carter, a guy named Doug, and another named Sherman. We had decided that we wanted to make money in order to more fully enjoy our individual pleasures. We also wanted to purchase club jackets with our club name on it, which was the style back in the late forties and early fifties. One of the ways we made money was by giving "waistline" parties, which meant that anyone attending our party would pay a penny for whatever his or her waist was in inches. This money, plus the dues we paid, we would put into our treasury and continue to build it up so we could buy our flashy jackets. Well, that day never arrived, thanks to our treasurer, Sherman, whose books were not accurate, nor was his excuse for what happened to the money. So, with those dreams short-lived, the Marquis broke up, and we went back to doing what we did before: buying loose cigarettes for a penny apiece and drinking cherry Coke to kill the tobacco taste and smell; playing the usual street games of stickball and loadies; standing on the stoop and teasing passing girls; and trying to become winos.

I only had a momentary flirtation with becoming a wino, which was simply an attempt to be like the adults I saw in the neighborhood. The problem was, Walter, Doug, and myself had only a vague idea of how to deal with drinking liquor, and we never thought we would get sick. Well, we did. When I got home, feeling very good but sick as hell, dinner was ready and I was expected to eat. If I didn't eat I would be subjected to a lot of questions I was not prepared to answer, so I ate a little—just enough to create a small inferno in my stomach and send me running to the bathroom. My loud vomiting had everyone concerned except Joe, who knew why I was sick and told Aunt Della. And, once again, Aunt Della did not punish me: the discomfort I was having was punishment enough. So much for becoming a wino.

That first year was filled with invaluable learning experiences, and very soon what Tallahassee roots I had brought with me had been replaced by New York ones. Aunt Della, and her introductions to a broader and more culturally entertaining way of life, was certainly a contributing factor. But there was also me. I was growing fast, both in body and in mind. Unfortunately, I had never learned to dance in Tallahassee, and in New York you *had* to dance, particularly at parties. I went to all the parties anyway, of course, and learned to fake a slow dance and to "grind." The grind was a popular dance at the time that involved leaning against a wall and moving sensuously against your partner—even I could do that. But I still had a long way to go on the next step: talking.

This was a real problem with girls. I was good at getting a girl's attention, but I couldn't hold it. One reason was my shyness, and another was the poor self-image I had of myself. All through my teen years and into my adult ones, I always had the fear of rejection. Not having nice clothes or enough money were excuses I made for my obvious inferiority complex. So I made the decision that if I was going to continue my active social life I would need money. That meant I would have to go to work.

One thing I decided I would not do was shine shoes, a career which ended the day I arrived in New York. But I had no hang-ups over delivering newspapers, so, thanks to my friend Walter Carter, I started delivering the New York newspapers, which was nothing like delivering papers in Tallahassee. There, I delivered in the afternoon, after school. But in New York I had to get up at 5 A.M. and deliver my papers before I went to school. Sunday papers were a chore, too. They were as thick as a classified directory, and it took many trips to complete my deliveries, which became one of the reasons I eventually gave up this job. The other was the snow and the winter, which could be real bad at times. It was hard to believe that I had spent many days wishing for snow in Tallahassee: snow to play in, not deliver newspapers in. It took only one winter in New York to help me decide that my newspaper delivery career should come to an end.

My next jobs were not any better, or easier, nor did they give me a lot of money for all the work involved. First I tried delivering groceries at the local supermarkets, but the tips were too little to compensate for the labor and time each delivery took. After that I got a job delivering ice, which was normal in those days since most people in my neighborhood could not afford a refrigerator. It was very hard work, which I was not unaccustomed to as I had been working since I was nine years old. It didn't matter how hard the work was as long as the end result was making money so I could buy something special.

The special need for money at that time was so I could buy a new trombone, the instrument I played in my junior high orchestra. Actually, I had one the school had loaned me, but that was used. And now that graduation was near many kids in the orchestra were making plans to attend the High School of Music and Art, a top school for those serious about music, which I felt I was. Most of my schoolmates had their own instruments for the test, and I felt I could never pass the music performance if I didn't have my own instrument as well. Of course, I wasn't being totally honest with myself: I was trying my best to block out the fact that I had remained in the school band by the skin of my teeth, and that I really wasn't that proficient on the trombone. Also, my original reason for joining the orchestra was to be near Hazel, who played the flute, and because the orchestra often went on field trips. But my inferiority complex wouldn't let me accept the truth. I was dead certain that all I needed was my own trombone to pass the test and be accepted.

That was the reason I accepted Wallace's invitation to spend the summer of 1950 in Tallahassee; I felt I could convince him to buy my trombone. The problem was, Wallace had his own plans for me: he wanted me to move back to Tallahassee. And if I did I would be the recipient of a new motor scooter. It was a tempting offer, which was made difficult by the fact that I had become a thorough New Yorker by this time, and Tallahassee to me was someplace I had once lived, that's all. However, I couldn't get the scooter out of mind, so I thought I'd ask Ruby if she felt like having me move closer to her in Orlando, where she still lived.

"Boy," Ruby said in her very direct and no-nonsense way,

"if you don't get yourself back to New York, I'll come to Tallahassee and drag you back." Ruby always had a way with words, and because she was a woman of her word, I returned to New York at the end of the summer without a new trombone.

What at first seemed like a setback to me was really an opportunity to advance as a person. I was now left with a decision which I had to make: whether to continue telling myself that I was proficient enough to try for Music and Art, or look for another high school, and one that would be beneficial to me and my future career. Well, after talking with several other recruiters, I chose Food Trades Vocational High School because the recruiter there said the magic words: "Cooks make a lot of money."

It didn't matter that I had never thought of myself as a cook, or that I might have made a flimsy, narrow-minded decision based on my obsession with money. It was *my* decision, and based on what *I* wanted for me. Neither Wallace, Ruby, nor Aunt Della told me what to decide. They in their respective ways did influence me, but the ultimate final decision was mine. I was now a lot more ambitious and independent, and was no longer the nervous, naive kid who shuddered whenever Ruby raised her voice. Whether that was true or not was going to be determined when I faced Ruby, who had finally made plans to join me in New York.

3

Hatred is like an acid. It can do more damage to the vessel in which it is stored than it can to the object on which it is poured.

Ruby's arrival in New York, after three years of not being exposed to her fiery ways, caused a little anxiety for me. I felt sure she was going to invade the life and style of living I had become accustomed to. And if she did, I knew it would not be a happy reunion.

Well, my fears were without merit because Ruby's arrival was a happy event, and a family reunion of sorts since Ruby's mother, Grandma Julia, made the move with her. Also, my graduation from junior high school was one of pride and happiness. And there was the transition from Aunt Della's hospitality to living once again with Ruby, which wasn't too bad because after fifteen years I was finally going to have my own room.

It was not, however, a private room, since everyone had to pass through it to get to the bathroom and kitchen. But that two-bedroom apartment in Harlem was the best that could be found in a short time and in our price range. Located on 149th Street and Eighth Avenue, it reminded me of the railroad flat we lived in in Tallahassee, and had none of the residential feeling of Aunt Della's neighborhood, which was twelve blocks away. I was now a resident of Harlem, which is truly a black metropolis, and being black didn't mean instant acceptance by

the community. It was then—and still is—a world unto itself.
There is every conceivable kind of person and every kind of
business, everything from numbers runners to pimps and prosti-
tutes, from large churches with huge congregations to store-
front churches. And there was Manny's Pool Hall, located at
the street level of our apartment building, which was my favorite hangout, especially when playing hooky from high school.

Ruby was very productive from the moment she hit New
York, finding the apartment right away. But she was more concerned about finding employment doing the thing she knew
best, domestic work. Grandma Julia decided not to work, since
that would mean going out in the Harlem streets, which she
was deathly afraid of. Actually, my sometimes cantankerous
grandmother, who was in her early fifties, was unskilled and il-
literate. Anyway, Ruby had decided that if she got a job her salary, plus the money from my pickup jobs, would be enough to
get us through. She did not find a job right away, however,
which almost ruined her plans.

But then a job did come her way, and for very good pay.
The conditions of the job, though, were lousy. She worked for
a family in Forest Hills, Long Island (which was not too far by
subway from Harlem), named the DuFines—Irving and Doris,
and four young daughters whose ages were from ten years to an
infant. Ruby liked the family but not the request that she be a
live-in domestic. That was not what she had bargained on,
since she had a family of her own. She took the job, though,
after she realized how much could be saved buying groceries
for two instead of three, and that Forest Hills was not the end
of the world. Besides, I could visit her on weekends, and she
would come to our home on Thursdays, which is the National
Day Off for all domestics.

So Ruby started her new employment as a live-in with the
DuFines, and that September of 1951 I started my new school,
Food Trades Vocational High School, which I enjoyed very
much. I felt like an adult going to work, since I rode the subway every day. And in a way it was a job, making new friends
and acclimating myself to high school procedures and termi-
nology. But it was fun, stockpiling recipes and learning my way

around the school's well-equipped kitchen. It required my full concentration. My school days were divided between my vocational training and my academic subjects, which were not a priority in a vocational school. In our second year we were put into a work-experience class, which meant we alternated a week of school with on-the-job training. And it also meant that we got paid for the week of OJT, which I liked best of all.

I was assigned to the pantry of the Essex House Hotel, one of the important hotels in downtown Manhattan, but I wasn't happy about the assignment. I thought I would be placed behind the ranges cooking the main dishes, but what they had me doing was preparing salads, desserts, pancakes, and waffles. And, although I got to wear the white chef's uniform, I could not wear the hat since I was not behind a range. I felt that if I were ever going to qualify for the highest money as a cook I needed to get my training at the chef level. So I took my complaint to my counselor. I was told the pantry was temporary, and since I was already in the kitchen I would be first in line when an opening came up behind the ranges. That was encouraging, so I took the pantry job and became the best pancake maker at the Essex House, a skill and meal I fell back on many times in the years to follow.

After a year I realized that my counselor's words of encouragement were only that, because when there were openings behind the range they were given to two white students who had started school after me and my alternate, Robert Williams, who was also black.

I was discouraged, to say the least, and I felt that racism was the reason I didn't get what I deserved. It hurt me. Therefore, I started thinking again about whether I really wanted to be a cook. And as I thought more about it, how I had been encouraged with a lie, I became more discouraged. But, worst of all, I gave up my commitment to a career as a cook, at which I felt I could have been the very best.*

I didn't give up the Essex House, however, because I needed the money. But I lost interest in school and found ref-

---

* In retrospect I feel because my original commitment to a career as a cook was not total, I was destined to fail.

uge at Manny's Pool Hall. It was a confusing period for me, made worse by my Grandma Julia, who was uncommunicative and didn't seem to care what was happening to me, or whether I came home or not. So I stayed away, and would come in late every night. Aside from Manny's, I would frequent the movie theaters in Times Square, and whatever reliability and trust I possessed before seemed to disappear when I was no longer committed to school. This was certainly true the time Ruby gave me some money to pay the telephone and electricity bills, but I went to Manny's instead, thinking I could increase it playing pool. I thought I was a good pool player, but I wasn't good enough, obviously, because I lost every cent of the money. I also lost any courage I had to tell Ruby what I had done, and take the punishment. Instead, I put my tail between my legs, so to speak, and ran.

But I wasn't running away. I simply chose the only place I figured I could go and hide for a while, and that was the subway. Since the subway ran twenty-four hours, it was perfect, but it was also a terrifying experience. I was sixteen years old, and I had been through a lot since coming from Tallahassee, but one thing I had never encountered was a homosexual. And late in the night when I was on the subway train alone, a lonely homosexual boarded the train I was in. This person didn't waste any time propositioning me, and I was scared to death. So I decided to act macho, feeling that might help to hide my fear. And I carried on this way all the time this person talked to me. Then, when the train stopped at a station, I hurried off. I felt good that I had gotten away. However, I could not escape the fact that I had stayed out all night, something I had never done before, and that renewed the fear in me of what would happen when Ruby found out.

The only thing that eased my fears about Ruby was the fact that she was working, and I was sure Grandma Julia wouldn't miss me. So, after my all-night subway ride, I went to school the next morning. By now I was feeling pretty good. Then, about halfway through my first class, I was summoned to the principal's office, and my weary body became gripped with fear. On my way there I kept trying to think up some good excuse to keep the wrath of Ruby from destroying me when we met.

When I arrived at the principal's office, Ruby wasn't there, but she was waiting to speak to me on the telephone. It seemed Grandma Julia was not as unattentive to my comings and goings as I had thought, because she had called Ruby when I didn't come home. And even though talking to Ruby on the telephone was better than seeing her, I still feared Ruby's voice. But she surprised me; she was calmer than I had ever known her to be in a situation like this, and it was almost as effective as a beating. Because when I started to explain to her what had happened, I couldn't contain myself, and I broke down, emotionally. I was looking for sympathy and understanding when I broke down, and Ruby responded with some consoling words and the suggestion that I leave school and go home to get some rest.

That night, Ruby came home. We had a long talk and, much to my surprise, I was meeting a Ruby I didn't know. Somewhere in our period of separation—both while she was still in Florida and I in New York, and while she was living with the DuFines and I was living at home—she must have realized that I had grown up, because that's the way she was treating me. It was a nice experience, this new Ruby, who was trying with every word to let me know how much she loved me. And that I should avoid doing anything to upset her, but if I ever did I should own up to whatever it was that I had done. Since that time, Ruby's sage advice has been with me. But more important, I found out just how meaningful a relationship can be when people communicate with one another.

I also realized my life had a new lease, and that there was freedom to do things and to make decisions now that were not possible before with Ruby. So, thinking of her wishes, I went back to school, regularly, but only to get my diploma, because I still had no idea what I wanted to be. And along about this time my best friend, Walter Carter, who had joined the Air Force, came home on leave from two months' basic training. I was impressed with the reception he received, and how good he looked in his blue Air Force uniform made me envious enough to find out as much as I could about the Air Force, since I was still searching for a direction to take.

It was an identity I was really looking for, and without any direction I was quite impressionistic, especially when it came to something that one of my friends had done. I was impressed that he had found something to escape to, which I wanted also. But had I been a lot more mature about such things, I would have realized that all I needed was already inside me. I should have been thinking about what was best for *me*, and going after it. Instead, I chose the Air Force because I no longer wanted to attend high school, and it also sounded good to me.

I immediately began putting together all the answers to the questions I was sure Ruby would ask. One immediate problem was my age; I was not going to be seventeen years old for a couple of months, so I needed Ruby's consent. Also, joining up would mean I would leave school with only a year to go. This bothered me, until an Air Force recruiter I went to see explained to me how I could finish high school in the service. The other helpful tale I could tell Ruby, and one that impressed me as well, was that the Air Force would send me to school to teach me a trade. So, now that I was fortified with all the answers, I went to Ruby. She didn't fight it or ask any questions—maybe because I answered every one she might have asked before she asked it. At any rate, on July 1, 1953, when I turned seventeen years old, Ruby signed for me to join the U.S. Air Force.

It's funny. No matter how fast you want to do something, it will never happen until it is to happen. Such was the situation with me after I had signed up to go into the Air Force, taken the physical, and had my bag packed. True, some of the delay was because my physical examination had indicated I might have a heart murmur. That was soon corrected by some additional tests. But after four months I was starting to feel it was not going to happen, just like getting behind the range at the Essex House, and I was about to change my mind. Then those magic words, "Greetings," arrived, and I was told to report for induction on November 13, 1953. It was official. And even though I was going to start this new life on Friday the thirteenth, I didn't care.

Besides, I wasn't going very far away—about 271 miles from New York City, to be exact—near a city called Geneva, New York. This was where Sampson Air Force Base was located, and where I would spend the next two months undergoing basic training. When I left on the bus for Sampson I was given a farewell by Ruby and Aunt Della, which was quite appropriate. After all, the two people who had contributed the most to who I was now should take a last look, so to speak, before I entered this new phase of my life.

Part of the reason I had joined the Air Force was to fly, be around airplanes, and see the world. I soon found out Sampson was not going to make that a reality, not for me or any of the hundreds of other raw, frightened young men like me. Instead, we would spend the next two months being deprogrammed from our civilian way of life. And the first thing on the agenda was to strip us of all human dignity and make us feel smaller than small. One way was in the clothing; they would issue you clothing that was far too large for you. And if you complained about what their tailor had issued you, then you could expect to be yelled at regularly. It was their philosophy that the more yelling we experienced the stronger would be our sense of fear. Hell, I was way ahead of them. Ruby had preceded them by seventeen years.

Some of the basic training techniques were also set up to make you feel homesick. Here again that was no problem for me, because once I thought about where I had come from it only made me glad to be at Sampson, at least for a change. So a lot of their demands really made me feel right at home, like the one about keeping our shoes "spit" shined. Since I started in that business at an early age, and left while I was still young, I still had a large supply of spit left. About the only part of basic training I hadn't learned from Ruby was marching, guard duty, learning to fire a gun, and war maneuvers—although I did have to maneuver away from Ruby on some occasions when she was on the warpath. But I was not too keen about guns, since I had never been in the same room with one. Having one, or using one, had never been on my list of necessities. The Air Force had their own ideas, and so I learned to fire—plus disassemble and assemble—an M-16 carbine. That, incidentally, was my first and last time firing any kind of weapon.

After a month the Air Force must have decided to test their deprogramming, because we received our first passes to leave the base. And we must have passed the test since there were additional passes to come, plus overnight privileges. It was on these excursions into Geneva that I was introduced to the art of topless dancing and my first fling with alcohol. It's true, I had suffered when I became inebriated as a teenager, but that was from wine, not hard liquor. Nevertheless, I survived both experiences, and even established the first of a long list of favorite drinks I would have over the years. The only thing I remember about that drink was the color. It was pink, and the name of the drink is a blank, which is the way I would feel after consuming three of them. Although I survived my many drinking bouts with those pink whatchamacallits, I never really learned to handle the alcohol too well. It served mainly to pass the time while I stared at the topless dancers and wished my salary as an Airman Basic were more so I could afford them.

The war maneuvers, or war games, which signaled the end of basic training were not appealing to me, and I hoped I would never do them for real. By now I had gone from weighing 133 to 155 pounds in two months. I didn't know what to accredit those extra pounds to. But after being told that my next duty station—my technical training school—was in Mississippi, I figured I would need that weight, and maybe a few other things, to deal with that part of the world I thought I had seen for the last time in 1948.

When I arrived at Keesler Air Force Base in Biloxi, Mississippi, I had left the liberally cool climate of upstate New York to go to the hotbed of racism, Mississippi. I was now in one of the chief locations which made up the "Cotton Curtain," so called because of the rigid segregation laws for black people. This was January 1954, and Dr. Martin Luther King, Jr., had not yet set his civil rights boll weevils loose in the "Cotton Curtain." Therefore I made up my mind that for my nine months at Keesler I would stay out of the way of those people who didn't like me because I was black, and I hoped they would do likewise for me.

In any case I was going to have my hands full learning to repair airplane radar and radio equipment. Somehow my aptitude test told the Air Force that I was qualified to do that kind of work, although math was my worst and most disliked subject throughout my entire school career. But I didn't complain about what the Air Force felt my capabilities were: hell, I didn't know, so how could I tell them they were wrong? Besides, I thought there might be a future for me since television was now getting bigger, and more families were owning sets.

Television became one of my pastimes on the base when I wasn't attending my classes. Actually, going to school at Keesler was like going to college. Military life was not as demanding as at Sampson, meaning there was some marching, some inspections, and a great emphasis on academics and the technical. There were also some pretty nice airmen, both white and black, whom I became friends with. It was the white airmen who took the seriousness out of segregation one day as a show of their friendship toward me, and to prove that where there's solidarity there is a way to overcome even segregation.

The solidarity between the white airmen and me had developed at Sampson, where we went through basic training together. They were quite liberal in their thinking, and we had developed a camaraderie in basic training which saw us all going out together, often. So it was not out of the question that the same should prevail at Keesler, despite the segregation laws, which bugged them. Therefore my white airmen friends got the bright idea that we should all go into town together. And the way that would be done—so as to avoid the segregated bus that went to town—was for all of us to take the same taxicab. Their intentions were good, although they were not thinking ahead, like what would happen once we were in town on foot. We couldn't go into any of the entertainment houses together, because if we did we'd end up in jail, or worse. I couldn't subject them to that, nor did I want to put myself in that kind of jeopardy. I had joined the Air Force to learn a trade, see the world, and not to die in the South.

Another reason why I was better off finding something to do on the base was because most of my meager salary was being sent home to Ruby. What was left for me barely took care of my desire to gamble. But I did gamble on picking up some money from Wallace, whom I visited on a few occasions since I had a friend who drove to Florida on some weekends. But I should have remembered the situation with the trombone, because Wallace was no more generous now that I was on my own and making a living, so to speak. He felt I should pay my own way, that I should always be responsible for whatever I wanted. It was a good lesson for me to learn, I later realized; one that I now try to share with my sons.

After a while I stopped making those Florida trips. However, it did spark a need in me to get off the base more, a spark that almost turned to lightning on a few occasions. Like the time I ventured ten miles outside of Biloxi to a hangout in a city called Gulfport. It was like finding a lost city, very few people ever went there, and those who lived there never left. And strangers weren't that welcome, although I was left alone. What eventually ran me out of this place was a test of my motto: Avoid danger if I know where it's going to be. One night some wild shots were fired in this backwoods club I frequented. That was enough to cancel my trips to Gulfport.

Eventually, I decided to try Main Street in Biloxi, which was the black part of town, and right across the railroad tracks. It was in this area that I discovered a new favorite drink, Early Times whiskey and Coke. And, like most drinks I tried, I always consumed more than I could handle. I was in a period of trying to challenge booze, with me always the loser, because I would end up flat on my backside. However, Main Street was also where I had my first sexual experience. It was due to happen, considering the number of aborted attempts while growing up in New York. I needed a shot at the real thing to complete this development into manhood that was happening in the Air Force, and a sexy young waitress named JoAnne made it possible. About the same time I completed my training at Keesler, and not a moment too soon as far as I was concerned.

During my nine months at Keesler I had come into my own. I had also managed to get through technical school, and whether I had learned anything or not would be found out at my first duty station, Hickam Air Force Base, Honolulu, Hawaii. This assignment was a pleasant surprise, having spent nine months in Mississippi. However, I was slightly skeptical about Hawaii because the rumors were that it was "as bad as Mississippi" if you were black. But then, rumors ran rampant in the military, and this was just one of many I had heard. The fact that I had two weeks' leave before reporting for departure was all I thought about, and I even skipped dinner at Keesler to catch the first thing smoking out of town to New York.

What that turned out to be was a back-of-the-bus Greyhound to Mobile, Alabama, where I would catch an airplane and leave behind that world of segregation. But there would be one more reminder. Since I had not eaten at the base I was plenty hungry when I got to Mobile. However, if I wanted to eat, it would have to be at the back door of the kitchen, "where colored are served." I had had it with the back of everything, and since going home meant Ruby's home cooking, I decided to stay hungry a little longer. Unfortunately, I did not have the control over my bladder that I had over my stomach. Therefore, I was forced to use the segregated rest rooms.

When I got home I had my home-cooked meal. It was shared with two other men living with Ruby, her two grandsons, Joseph Hall and Lucius Hall, Jr. Ruby, in her younger days, had some reckless times, with the results being Lucius, Sr., who was also known as "Buster," and was seven years older than I.

My nephews were not the only change I found at home. A fire had forced Ruby to move to the Bronx, to a basement flat which was smaller and cheaper. Grandma Julia was now living with Aunt Della and Uncle Fred, who had hit the numbers, big, and had purchased a three-story apartment building. I was greeted like a hero when I returned home after eleven months, with everyone telling me how nice I looked in my Air Force threads, and how much I had changed. Actually, I was just a year older—eighteen years old, now—with some experiences I couldn't share, and I still had a lot of growing up to do in a lot of ways, which were not apparent to me then. What was apparent was the six days I had to live it up before grabbing a train to the West Coast.

And it was a good thing I already had my train ticket, because after I finished being a big shot my pocket money had been reduced to two dollars. However, I wasn't concerned about my overspending, since there was the joint savings account Ruby and I had, and to which two thirds of my salary had been going all the time I was away. I just knew I could get what I needed from it. Wrong. Ruby had not changed, even if I had. And when I left New York for California it was with a shoebox full of food, my same two dollars, and no one to see me off at the train station. So now my next lesson in being on my own was "making do" with what I had.

Therefore my five days of travel by train took some careful planning of both budget and food. But even with all my planning, by the time I reached San Francisco I was broke and hungry. So my first stop, before continuing on to Travis Air Force Base, which was fifty miles away, was at the USO. There I loaded up on stale, tasteless doughnuts, which did taste good because I was so hungry. They were enough to hold me until I could get to chow at Travis, which was at midnight. From then on it was just a matter of days before I was on my way to Hawaii.

It took five long days to reach Hawaii via troopship. This was my first sailing on the high seas, just as the flight from Rochester to Mobile, that got me to Biloxi, was my first airplane ride. It was not easy avoiding seasickness and doing a balancing act during one of the rougher moments on the ocean. Therefore, when the beautiful shores of Hawaii were sighted, I was happy, but there was some trepidation; Hawaii was the first "foreign country" I had been to, I told myself at the time.

Shortly after I got settled in Hawaii, I realized my anxieties were unnecessary. For instance, the rumor I had heard about Hawaii being comparable to Mississippi, may have been valid for some blacks, but not for me. The closest, and the first, encounter I had with racism occurred some time after my arrival. Through a contest in a newspaper I won a series of dance lessons at the Arthur Murray Dance Studio in Honolulu. Since I had never managed to develop as a dancer, I felt this would be a great opportunity to finally let someone teach me. However, when I went to collect my prize I got the impression I was not what they expected. Nevertheless, I did mange to get one lesson out of them, even though it was given with much reluctance. It might have been racism, or it could have been that my instructor felt I was putting her on. After all, it was a known fact then, just as now, that *all* blacks have rhythm and can dance.

As for the "foreign country" feeling I had, that was dispelled quickly. The only thing foreign in Hawaii was anyone who did not fall in love with this paradise. And being in the Air Force at Hickam Field was another phase of military life I had not expected. I lived in the barracks, but I had my own room and all the privacy I had never had at home. And the work I had been trained for at Keesler wasn't difficult at all. I was placed on the swing shift (4 P.M. to midnight), repairing radio and radar equipment on C-97 and C-124 aircraft. The work was not bad at all. In fact it got down to my repairs being nothing more than a good swift kick to the equipment if it failed. Funny, they never taught us that technique at Keesler.

With my military hours set, I was able to go out and find a part-time job, mainly because I never had any money since Ruby was still getting most of my pay. I found a job in the cafeteria of the air terminal on Hickam, which was operated by a civilian firm. My duties varied from busing tables to washing dishes to soda jerking to short-order cooking to driving the delivery truck, since I had managed to learn how to drive.

What I really managed to do was not destroy all the aircraft at Hickam, because my driver's training was during my working hours, and on an aircraft tug. The closest I had come to driving was from the passenger side, so that when I started teaching myself things got to be a bit hazardous. But I managed. And as soon as I could afford it I decided to get my own wheels.

Well, that decision was easy enough to make, but my choice of cars was the worst. And like most new drivers—and young ones for sure—I didn't care what kind of car I got. I just wanted my own wheels! That's just about all I got when I bought a 1941 Pontiac, which I kept for a minute more than its life expectancy. I had to push it all the way to the dealer when I traded it in for a flashy 1954 white Ford convertible, which made me the coolest airman on the base, I thought. But it also became my nemesis. Almost immediately after I started driving this car on base I started collecting traffic violations, and my driver's permit had expired. Eventually I was caught by the base Air Police, tried and court-martialed, which resulted in my losing one of my two stripes and a lot of money by being reduced a grade. But that was only the beginning, and a warning I refused to heed.

My next problems had nothing to do with my flashy white convertible, although it would play an indirect role in the eventual outcome of this period of trouble. It began one day when I was going to work with two other friends, and we spotted this shapely blonde dressed in a white outfit. We were so pleased by what we were seeing that we acknowledged her with a couple of whistles. After we laughed at what we had done, I went for a test flight in a C-124. Upon my return from the test flight, I was taken into custody by the Air Police. It seems the lady we had whistled at was the wife of an Air Policeman, who was also a native of Alabama, and he had not liked the "disrespect" shown his wife, for which I was singled out. Therefore I was harassed, threatened, and told I had better watch my step on base. Also I was told by the officer in charge of the Air Police that I was not being singled out because of my color, only because of what I had done. I found that hard to believe since no one seemed to mind that the two other airmen had also whistled.

After that warning I did move very carefully, and I would even see the Alabama Air Policeman, who *was* keeping an eye on whatever I did on base. Then, some time after I thought everything might be better, I decided to drive my car—which I had left in the hands of a friend—when I still was not supposed to, and I was instantly picked up. I had broken the law and I paid the price. Once again I was court-martialed, thus losing the other stripe, and worst of all I was sentenced to thirty days in the stockade (military prison). It was hard to believe that all of this was happening to me, especially since I had managed to avoid run-ins with the law both in New York when I was growing up, and in Mississippi where my rights were less than in Hawaii.

But the sound of the cell door closing on me made me realize that what was happening to me was real. It was a degrading feeling, having to ask permission to do things that I could do before, freely, like going to the bathroom. I was humiliated. And I told myself that this would be the last time I ever broke the law. My words must have been heard by the Almighty, because after seven days my case was dropped and I was released. I also had my one stripe returned to me. The law had spoken, and said that I could not be tried twice for the same offense, which was driving without a proper permit. But, thinking back, I am convinced that my short period in that stockade, and the resulting humiliation, was God's way of teaching me a lesson. Well, it worked: I learned my lesson.

After my release I sold the cause of part of my problems, the white convertible. But the truth is, *I* was the cause of my own problems, not some car or person. I could have avoided everything that happened to me. However, I didn't realize this until I found myself in another form of incarceration, on an island in the Pacific called Guam. It was really a tiny atoll, and perfect for doing a lot of reassessing, as well as drinking, gambling, and killing a lot of mosquitoes while trying to kill a lot of time. It was what the military called "temporary duty," and it lasted for eighty-six days, a lot longer than my stockade stay. And I even had the feeling that this duty was the Air Force getting even with me for getting out of my previous incarceration early. It was almost as bad, what with the lack of social life on Guam. But there was enough liquor to drink, and a lot of gambling.

And with my love of gambling, I was drawn in easily. I also was luckier than I had ever been, especially with the dice. I made bundles of money, and I spent it all on myself, Ruby, and Aunt Della. I bought jewelry for them and some shirts and tailored slacks for myself, plus five bottles of V.O. whiskey—my favorite drink at this time—to take back with me to Hawaii. By now I was what they call a "serious drinker," but not an alcoholic. I was getting there, and something dramatic needed to happen to make me stop.

There had been many times when I did say to myself, "If I had only stopped," which was always after I had drunk too much and felt sick, or after I had lost all of my money gambling. I was really ridiculous when it came to gambling, especially not knowing when to stop. It should have been when I was winning. But I would not. I would continue playing until I had lost all my money. Then I would borrow money against my skimpy paycheck and lose that. My drinking habit I credit to military life, it being an indigenous part of that life. With many military personnel in the service, drinking is the first order of business once the off-duty hours begin. My off-duty hours were spent the same way. On one of these occasions I tried a screwdriver—vodka and orange juice—for the first and last time. This friend of mine would mix them in a one-gallon mayonnaise jar for everyone, but not for me. I stayed away from screwdrivers because of the potency of vodka. However, after some coaxing, I tried one. I gulped it down and responded with, "This is nothing but orange juice, gimme another one." Well, there were four more: enough to turn my legs to rubber and bring on nonstop vomiting. That was my last screwdriver but not my last bout with alcohol.

By the time I was ready to leave Guam I was drinking a fifth of alcohol at a time with one or more friends. So the five bottles of V.O. I bought to take back to Hawaii were some "friends" I needed since I had no social life, nor did I see one happening when I returned to Hawaii. That day, when the plane landed at Hickam Field, four of the five bottles of V.O.

broke. I almost cried over the loss of my "friends." What I should have done, maybe, was to look at that loss as my gain— or even an omen. I should have made that one remaining bottle of alcohol my last, because it could have been my end.

I didn't observe the omen, but I did reduce my alcohol consumption. My love life seemed to open more than it had before I went to Guam. There was, however, a problem of inexperience. I would never approach women with seduction in mind, and that might have been because I just didn't know how to communicate with the opposite sex. But I continued to try. And finally I succeeded when I met a girl named Laila, a black girl who had been raised by a Hawaiian family since she was a small child. I spent a lot of time with Laila, who I had decided was my dream girl; she was certainly one of the few girls I had become serious about since leaving Tallahassee.

And with everything else, there was another side of me which suddenly came out: the humorous side. All of a sudden I became a practical joker and a prankster. Whatever the reason, I found fun in doing things like unfurling rolls of toilet paper from the top of the stairs of our four-story barracks, or deflating the tires of all the officers' cars in the parking lot. And there were other things which were equally crazy and terribly silly. I was just having a good time and not taking very much too seriously. Hawaii had also gotten to me, and I started thinking of it as someplace I wouldn't mind living once my time in the Air Force was up. Well, that would have to be dealt with later, because my time in Hawaii was up, and I was being sent back to California for discharge, which would be in six months.

The information that I would have to leave Hickam Air Force Base was a heartbreaking piece of news, the first duty station I had ever regretted leaving. Obviously my feelings had something to do with my own change of personality. Just as I had found what I should have found earlier—a new life-style, a love for Hawaii, and a girl there I loved—I was being taken away from it all. Therefore I made up my mind I would return to Hawaii after my discharge, and after I had gotten a last look at New York City.

My six months at Travis Air Force Base were easy. There were no really serious military activities that I had to get involved with. So my time was mostly my own. Most of this time was used to visit San Francisco, and the rest was spent completing my high school education, for which I took the high school equivalency test. This got me a General Equivalency Diploma, which I felt would help me get a job when I returned to Hawaii. I was glad that I had the time to get my high school diploma, because that was one of the things I had told Ruby could be done in the Air Force. And since I was returning after four years with news that I would be leaving again, I thought the least I could bring home was a high school diploma. It was also a symbolic release from Ruby, just as my honorable discharge was my release from the Air Force.

4

The most constant thing in life is change.

That November day in 1953 when I left New York City, high school, Ruby, and a life which didn't seem to be going anywhere to join the Air Force, I didn't know if I would ever return. For sure, I hoped I would return a lot better off than I had left. However, four years later I was back where I had started, the only difference being that I was now twenty-one years old, a bit more mature, a seasoned gambler, reformed drinker, and unemployed. I also had a more independent attitude, which could turn out to be a reason for Ruby and me to clash, especially if she still insisted that I was her "little boy." Therefore I would have to convince her to think of me as just her son.

What I didn't have to convince Ruby to do when I returned to New York was let me be a free boarder until I found a job. Ruby had made yet another move since I had last been home and was now living in a two-bedroom apartment in Aunt Della's and Uncle Fred's building in the Bronx. Ruby's younger sister, Aunt Lillie, was sharing the apartment, so some changes were in order to accommodate me. Aunt Lillie got the master bedroom, Ruby converted the dining room into her bedroom, and I got the tiny but private smaller room. This was my first room in a family house that was not shared with someone or used as a throughway.

It was, basically, a good arrangement for everyone, including Grandma Julia, who was already living with Aunt Della and Uncle Fred in one of the other apartments. And Uncle Fred's renting to relatives he knew were responsible assured him of a steady income. But after he had hit the number, which had provided the money to buy this apartment building, he changed considerably. For one thing, he gave up banking numbers and got a job as a taxicab driver. He also learned how to repair television sets and was able to add to his income. But the most remarkable change, as far as I was concerned, was his becoming religious. He became a deacon in the Tried Stone Baptist Church in the Bronx, which must have affected Aunt Della, who was not a very religious person during my time with her. She gave up playing cards, a favorite game, to concentrate on taking care of Uncle Fred and their home. And as a landlady Aunt Della was pretty good. But during the winter months, which was when I returned home, she was a tyrant with the heat. Aunt Lillie and Ruby were accustomed to it. Since I had just returned from an always warm climate, I had hoped for a little warmer reception.

Nevertheless, returning home to my entire family was inspiring. I needed the support of a family unit, even though Grandma Julia was still a bit uncommunicative. And Ruby was still the same, domineering, but with one exception: she could no longer give me beatings. I also was able to get back to my favorite cookies, Aunt Della's chocolate chip cookies. It took no time at all for me to renew my obsession with those very special morsels.

After a couple of weeks at home, that strong desire to return to Hawaii disappeared. I'm sure being around my family again had something to do with it. But I'm also sure that I was feeling some anxiety about being a civilian in Hawaii, without the Air Force or my own family support to fall back on should I find myself unemployed. Also, being with my family, I found I wanted to do more for them. Staying in New York, instead of returning to Hawaii, was one of my decisions. Another contributing factor in that decision was that Ruby did not exert any pressure on me to go to work, nor did I have to make any decisions about my future right away. But, knowing her as I did, I decided to beat Ruby to the punch, so to speak. I decided I would do something about my future before she brought it up.

And in less than a month after my return home I was working and scheduled to start school in order to enhance my future. Today I view those series of events as important to whatever success I have had. I didn't have the insight then to realize that your everyday activities are successes in their own right, but they are. Hell, just getting through each day is a tremendous success.

About the same time I started planning my future, I remembered someone from my recent past. A girl named Monya Dowdell, whom I had met in the Air Force when she was a WAF (Women in the Air Force), was from New York and had been discharged. I remembered her as a very bright and aggressive person. She was also the possessor of big expressive eyes and a big laugh that complimented her sense of humor. And I was lucky to have her phone number, because my call to Monya turned out to be a very important one. She was helpful in clearing up a vagueness in my mind as to what direction I should take when she suggested I do what she was doing and go back to school.

Monya was attending Collegiate Secretarial Institute, a business school located in New York City. She also explained that I could attend school on the GI Bill since I was a veteran, and that I would be paid while learning: a situation almost like my Food Trades/Essex House days. It seemed like a good idea to me, so I enrolled at Collegiate that December 1957, but I was not able to start classes until the new semester in January. However, Collegiate started working for me before I started working at Collegiate.

Collegiate was owned by Sadie Brown, who I believe was in her sixties. Mrs. Brown was short physically, but a giant in compassion and understanding. If you were serious about learning there was nothing she would not do to help you achieve your objective. If you were not, she would not hesitate to ask you to leave Collegiate. She was a woman of strong principles.

Along with Mrs. Brown's leadership, there were benefits to be derived from Collegiate's placement service. They guaranteed the students a job after successful completion of the courses. However, I was able to find out just how effective the placement services were before I had started classes. Lee Myers, Mrs. Brown's sister, was the reason why, and through her I began to realize the importance of personal relationships.

Lee, a younger and taller version of Mrs. Brown, had the trust and confidence of personnel directors at most of the major corporations in New York City. On her word alone she could place you with one phone call. This must have been the case when she informed me of a temporary job in the supply department at Saks Fifth Avenue during the Christmas holidays. This would hold me until January when I would start at Collegiate, at which time Lee promised me another job. If you were one of Lee's favorites, which I eventually became, and didn't like your job, she would find you another. Lee Myers was an important person in my life and future. By the confidence she expressed in my ability to perform, and also by the high recommendations she gave me, she forced me to try for excellence.

My job classification at Saks was stock clerk in the supply department. My duties were unloading packing cartons from trucks, in addition to receiving and storing packing and office supplies. I would also police the areas where cartons were stored to make sure they were neatly stacked, as well as deliver packing and office supplies to various departments. I did my duties with a fervor and enthusiasm that seemed as if my life depended on the outcome. And to a great degree, I suppose, it did.

I have come to believe that the end results of your life are based on the total sum of everything you have experienced. Therefore I believe the success I enjoy today is directly related

to my days at Saks Fifth Avenue. If I had not performed at my
highest level of competence, then I wouldn't be having a very
happy and brown day every day of my life today.

My commitment to excellence and being responsible, plus
my working hard, had positive results. Ernie Riccio, the manager of the supply department, arranged for me to continue at
Saks after the Christmas holidays. The only problem with continuing there were the hours. My schedule at Collegiate called
for me to attend afternoon classes. As far as my GI Bill was
concerned, attending afternoon classes was considered a full-
time educational load, and I received maximum financial support. I didn't want to give that up, and Saks decided they
didn't want to give me up. Therefore I was allowed to continue
working in the morning before my afternoon classes, and I was
also given additional hours in the evening after my classes,
bringing my weekly hours to forty. This helped my money
needs, and it was something Saks had never done for any employee.

I was honored and felt a sense of responsibility to Saks for
what they had done for me. Not only had they made it possible
for me to work a forty-hour week, I was left to supervise and
create work for myself. It gave me all the reasons I needed to
show more initiative, something Ernie had already seen when
he made his recommendations on my behalf. And Ernie eventually increased my responsibilities, as well as my education in
business. He explained every procedure in the department and
then had me meet and make friends with the various vendors
doing business with Saks. In other words, Ernie, an excellent
teacher, was preparing me for a career in business which would
benefit both Saks and me, if I were serious.

Attending Collegiate would provide me with the torch
that could show me the way to the end of the tunnel. The subjects were quite different from any I had ever had. There were
accounting, business, law, English, typing, shorthand, and a
brief course in money and banking, which was the most boring
I had ever experienced. My favorite subject was shorthand,

with accounting and typing tied for second. My shorthand teacher was able, through her great personality and her teaching style, to make shorthand come alive. She gave me the added incentive so important to students, making me feel I could actually master shorthand, and probably other subjects too. Despite my dislike for numbers, accounting and I got along fairly well. What I got involved in was trying to make the numbers balance and finding out the reason when they did not. I never wanted to be an accountant, but having gained a basic understanding of accounting proved useful when help was needed in balancing the financial problems of a new business.

As I had done with previous changes in my life, I made the adjustments of going to school and working smoothly and quickly. The Air Force had also helped me to adapt quickly to changing conditions and circumstances. When they said, "Move," you asked, "How far?" Some people refer to that kind of ability as "survivor instinct." It doesn't matter what anyone wants to call it, we should all possess that ability, because the most constant thing in life is *change*.

Thanks to work and school, my life seemed to be coming together. But part of that life was quite dull, I decided. Mostly it was all work and no play. I had no social life in between, and for my peace of mind—as well as my youthful needs—a change was necessary. Living in the Bronx, however, made that an easier desire than a practice, what with the amount of travel involved. For instance, there was the time I dated a girl who lived in Queens. I would have to travel by subway to pick her up, then we would go to a club, a concert, or a movie, usually all in Manhattan, before I took her home. Once there, I would spend some time trying to make out, before catching the subway for the long ride back to the Bronx. And each time it was exhausting. Therefore one of the first criteria I set for dating was that the girl had to live in the Bronx. Of course this did put a limitation on the number or variety of girls I might meet, but one snowy February evening in 1958 I did manage to meet someone special.

I attended a dance at Hunts Point Palace in the Bronx

with a high school chum named Robert Lambie. As things turned out, it became a very special occasion.

Lambie was meeting his girlfriend Shirley at the dance. And Shirley had brought a friend along named Maria La Forey who, in addition to living only three subway stops from me, was a very attractive and personable young lady. During our conversation I learned that she worked at Georg Jensen's, a fine silver and crystal store, which was only three blocks from Saks. Everything about Maria was quite convenient, plus we hit it off and began seeing each other regularly.

Maria also became my first full-time girlfriend. There had been other relationships, but they were short-term affairs. Maria became the real thing and made it official by telling her friends that the two of us were "going together"—two magic words which said a lot in those days, and these days too. And that's the way it was done at that time, just as we introduced each other to our families. When it got to that point, whatever thoughts may have been lingering about my returning to Hawaii's beautiful beaches and women was swept away by my burgeoning romance with Maria.

She was the youngest member of her family, which included three older brothers. She lived at home with her mother and two of her brothers. Maria's mother, Gladys—we called her "Aunt Gladys"—was a nurse, and was divorced, one more thing Maria and I had in common. Gladys was an active and independent person, and a fantastic cook, which meant I had many a home-cooked meal at Maria's house. And before I knew it I had acquired another family.

For the next several months, going into summer, Maria and I were inseparable. During that time we did the usual—going to parties, dances, the movies—and found pleasure in each other's body. Then, about July, Maria told me her period was late and she might be pregnant. We discussed it and decided to wait and see if things would change. I, however, became a little apprehensive about continuing the relationship. All during the nine months I had been out of the Air Force, there had never been any thought of marriage or children. However, I did enjoy being with Maria, and I decided I would continue seeing her. A few days after my decision she had her period.

The next month her period was late again. But this time Maria was pregnant. I don't know whether it was because the new life Maria had inside her was something I was responsible for, or what, but I told her we should get married. There had been no discussion or plans about marriage when we learned she was pregnant. It was just that I made up my mind that I was not going to be one of those guys who make a girl pregnant and then deserted her. My child would have my name and would not be born out of wedlock. Maria, however, did not agree. She did not feel I had to marry her just because she was pregnant. But I explained to her it wasn't just her being pregnant. I loved her, and eventually we would get married anyway. We were merely expediting what was inevitable.

Therefore the inevitable happened: Maria and I were married on Sunday, September 21, 1958, in a small private ceremony at the home of the pastor of the church Ruby and I attended. Our reception was small, with only family and a few friends, and was held at Wells Restaurant, located in Harlem, which was famous for its delicious chicken and waffles. Since it was Sunday, our reception ended early, and our honeymoon was spent in my tiny bedroom in Ruby's apartment because we both had to go to work the next day.

One thing I realized about marriage almost immediately was that there had been nothing in my life to prepare me for it. I don't mean my role of being a provider; having to work was, by now, second nature to me. And whatever I would be able to provide would depend on what my income allowed. Marriage, on the other hand, required a firm commitment, a firm partnership, and the giving of yourself to another human being. Well, at twenty-two years of age, I wasn't so certain I understood what that kind of commitment meant.

But despite my shortcomings our marriage proceeded along quite nicely. I continued to work and achieve at Saks, in addition to going to school, and Maria remained at her job until she was too far along in her pregnancy to continue. Then, about a month before she was due to have the baby, which was

my fifteenth month at Saks, Ernie recommended me to replace
him as manager of the supply department. He was being promoted and would now head up parcel post shipping. My approval for the job was an easy one since I impressed all those
casting a vote. I, however, was given the title of supervisor instead of manager, although I would be performing Ernie's same
duties. At least there was an increase in my salary, an amount I
can't recall, probably because it was not large. Whatever the
amount, it would be useful once the baby arrived.

My new title included executive status. What that meant
was a gold-colored identification card, a cash bonus at Christmas, and my standard employee thirty percent discount on all
merchandise. But, with the money I was making, the discount
did not bring me any closer to being able to buy at the place
where I worked. My new position cut my full-time afternoon
sessions, since I had to be at the store all day, to part-time
classes at night. This also decreased the amount of money I got
for going to school. But I did not let that deter me in my desire
to tackle my job with gusto.

Without the proper title, it was important to me that I
show my superiors I was "managerial material." So I attacked
the entire stockroom, which was maybe 1,500 square feet with
thousands of forms, and rearranged it. The room was given a
thorough cleaning by the clerks who worked with me, and I
worked as hard as they to make it the way I wanted it. I had
four clerks working with me, and I made the decision I would
always try to be fair, but firm, with them. Sometimes because
of my age—I was the youngest member of the crew—things got
a little sticky. But my not asking them to do anything I
wouldn't do made the difference, I feel.

Shortly afterward, Maria and I welcomed the arrival of
Michael Anthony, our first son, on Wednesday, April 1, 1959. I
was at work when the call came in, since I had dropped Maria
at the hospital earlier that morning.

Being the father of a newborn son created a feeling in me
I had never known. I was ecstatic when I got my first look at
Michael, and I did what so many thousands of other fathers
had done before me: I stared, made faces at Michael, waved at

him, and I let everyone know I was the father by pointing into the nursery and saying, "The one over there is mine." And I even attempted to see if Michael looked like me or Maria. That was nonsense because, as I and most parents have come to learn, newborn babies don't look like either parent—they look like themselves. But the most important thing was my realization that something very special had taken place. One day Michael was in Maria's stomach using her life-support system; the next day he was a brand-new human being with everything he would need to survive. To me, giving birth is one of the very definite proofs that there is a God. I read a quote that said, "A baby is God's opinion that the world should go on."

After a few days Maria and Michael were able to come home. That first day home I was able to hold him in the palms of my hands. He seemed so fragile I was afraid to handle him. And despite his tiny size, he made our tiny room seem even smaller, even though Michael's crib was one of our dresser drawers.

His living in tight quarters might have been the reason Michael was such a very good baby. Within a few weeks he was sleeping all night, which was a blessing to me who worked all day and went to school every night. And since he was the firstborn, he was everybody's pet, with me enjoying him the most. I became an expert at changing his diapers and bathing him once I got over the fear of breaking his tiny body, which was growing rapidly.

For a long time Maria and I had felt our tiny bedroom was closing in on us. But so was Ruby, who had her own ideas of how Michael should be raised. And so did Maria, whose West Indian stubbornness and strong will meant a showdown was not far off. Therefore I exercised my option to find a new apartment for me, Maria, and Michael. It was a fifth-floor, one-bedroom flat located in the Bronx near both of our parents. And it was far enough away from Ruby to give Maria the autonomy she needed with Michael, and to give me some peace of mind since I was having a rough enough time with work and going to school.

But after eight months the strain of working all day and

going to school at night proved to be more than I could handle. So I gave up school, even though I knew I would miss the extra money from the GI Bill. However, I had become totally immersed in my job at Saks, mostly because I felt I had a future there. I had also rationalized that what I was learning at Collegiate I would never use at Saks. But leaving Collegiate meant I would have to tell Mrs. Brown and Lee Myers, which was something I dreaded doing. After all, they had placed me with Saks, so my success was their success, I told myself.

Therefore my stopping school was a way to preserve the success I had already achieved at Saks. I came to this job with the intention of performing at the highest level for two reasons: to live up to the confidence Lee Myers had in me when she sent me to Saks, and to disprove the myth that black people were lazy and lacking in ambition. It wasn't that I saw myself as a pioneer for black rights, which were being handled very well by Dr. Martin Luther King, Jr., and the NAACP. I just felt I owed it to my race, and to myself, because I knew I was none of those things because my skin color was black.

And sometime later it seemed as though I was being looked at as someone with initiative, especially when the assistant general manager, Frank Sylvester, took a special interest in me. Mr. Sylvester felt that I could expand my horizons at Saks as a buyer. So he arranged for me to attend a retail and merchandising class at New York University, for which Saks paid. I liked the idea of his being interested in me and Saks paying for my growth, but after going to school for a while and wrestling with the math involved in retail and merchandising, I decided I didn't want to be a buyer.

About the same time I was making such great progress at work, I started having second thoughts about being married. It was probably having all the free time since I had stopped going to Collegiate, my new status, and feeling the grass was greener on the other side. "The other side" was some guys I was hanging out with who were footloose and fancy free, which I was not because I had a wife and child. Had I been a little more mature I would have realized that the grass was actually greener on my side.

Top left: Wallace Amos, Sr.

Side: Ruby Amos

Bottom: Wally Amos, sitting up all by himself at age six months.

Top right: The Mayday King of Lincoln Elementary-High School, age eight. By this time Wally had already learned all the books of the Bible. A friend said he looked like a fly in a glass of milk.

Bottom: Aunt Della (left) and Miss Amanda. At this point Aunt Della had no idea that she would inspire Wally to make the chocolate chip cookie a superstar . . .

Top: Wally and his junior high friends practicing facial expressions on the streets of Harlem.

Bottom left: At Keesler Air Force Base in 1954. Note the calculated crush in his hat — he's beginning to get into it.

Top left: Wally and Howard Hausman, his mentor at the William Morris Agency.

Bottom right: On the television set of "Black Omnibus," which starred James Earl Jones. Note the wash and wear clothing.

Nevertheless, being immature and still somewhat impressionistic, I started looking on the other side and began flirting with various ladies, eventually settling on one named Eula Armstrong. She was shapely and pretty, and also worked at Saks, which made things very convenient. Later there would be another affair, and with each such liaison my guilt increased along with my inability to communicate to Maria my true feelings. Thus the framework was laid for our first separation when Michael was two years old.

The reasons I gave Maria for leaving were that I no longer wanted to be married and that our marriage was not working; a pattern, I learned later in my life, I would repeat many times. The most difficult part of that leaving was Michael. His expression was one of trying to make sense out of something as a two-year-old that I, as an adult, could not find the words to make clear to his mother. Usually in a situation like this the partner staying thinks the partner leaving is feeling nothing about what he or she is doing. Well, that was not true with me. I was in pain—agonizing pain—because I knew I was hurting two people. And that pain was compounded because I didn't know of any other way to handle the situation.

Even moving in with Milton Duggins, a fellow worker at Saks who had his own apartment in Brooklyn, did not give me the answers. And because I seemed to need answers I did not enjoy my newfound freedom as much as I had thought I would. This was evident by how much I found I wanted to see and talk to Maria and Michael once I was gone, even though I saw Michael every weekend, and many evenings I would visit Maria to talk things over. Finally I reassessed what I had done. Had it been in haste? Was it an impulse? Had I made an honest and strong effort to make the marriage work? Those were the kinds of questions haunting my mind for the several weeks after I had separated from Maria. And each answer kept pushing me back to Maria and Michael, because I couldn't think about anyone else.

I went back home to Maria, but I didn't feel any different than when I had left. Somehow, not being there with them made me want to be there, but once I was there I wanted to be gone. And worst of all, I did not make a sincere effort to *want* to be there, or to try to make the marriage work. I simply went through the motions instead of being truthful with Maria. My other reason for being home—giving Michael a father at home —was a waste since my being there did not make it a happy home.

Affection, and being affectionate, was another area I was deficient in. I didn't know about being affectionate because I had not received very much myself. Therefore, how important affection was in a relationship was something beyond my understanding. And the only time we touched was when Maria and I made love; our sex life was about the only thing that kept us together. At any rate, I was back. For how long I didn't know.

My unhappiness was not merely confined to my home. I guess I needed something else to be unhappy with, so I became disenchanted with my job. When I gave up studying to be a buyer the supply department started looking like a dead end. In fact I saw it as not just a dead end but a low-paying dead end. I was making eighty-five dollars per week, which Saks thought was a good salary. I thought it needed improvement. My last increase, which was small, had been when I was promoted into Ernie Riccio's job with the understanding that I had to prove myself. Well, I had done that, and I wanted monetary recognition for doing a good job. And now that Maria was pregnant again, my eighty-five dollars needed support.

I had high hopes that I would get an increase, especially since I was only asking for ten dollars more per week. However, I was prepared to accept a counteroffer of half that amount, with the hope of better things to come. Well, Saks did not want to give me any false hopes, so they denied my request, including a counteroffer. Therefore I decided upon my next plan —which we'll call B—of giving Saks two weeks' notice. I figured this was the best way to let them know that I really meant business. Well, Saks held firm with their Plan A, of no increase, which meant I had to move forward with my Plan B.

It was now a matter of principle. I felt I was worth more than I was receiving, and for me to continue working for less than I deserved would have been against all I believed in. And heading the list of my beliefs was standing up for my worth. It was not my intention to let myself be abused.

So, with my wife pregnant, and with no sign of another job in sight, but my pride intact, on August 11, 1961—almost four years after joining Saks Fifth Avenue—I left at the end of the two weeks'. Saks did, however, thank me for my good work while there, and supported it with an excellent letter of reference, something I felt good about. Because once again I had terminated a relationship on good terms.

After I had terminated, I would periodically go back to Saks to say hello to a few friends. And on each of these occasions I realized how important it was that I had the courage to stand up for my worth, and that I had enough confidence in my ability to make a life-changing decision. You could say that I believed that there was more promise for me somewhere other than Saks, although where I did not know.

5

If it is to be, it is up to me.

The most logical thing to do after you quit your job—especially if you're married with one child and a second one on the way, and with no other job in sight—I did not do. It was because I didn't know what the logical thing to do was. I did know that I was tired, because I had not taken any time off in quite a while, and that I wanted to spend some time with Maria and Michael. I also needed some time to think about my future plans and to develop a course of action. Therefore I did what was logical to me: I took a week's vacation.

Once my brief vacation was over I dug into the New York *Times* classified section. I checked on everything that looked promising—a secretarial position because of my business school training, and management trainee positions because of my previous experience at Saks—but found nothing I liked. And after working for a week with the New York *Times* to find work, I decided to try something else, maybe a different kind of employment.

My thoughts turned to the Sanitation Department, which paid a salary of a hundred and fifty dollars or more per week. This was definitely more than I had made at Saks, and in 1961 you could live pretty good with that kind of money. I was tempted to do the sanitation work, but I started thinking about collecting garbage in ninety-degree heat during the summer, shoveling snow in the freezing winter, and never feeling that I had made a contribution to anything but my pockets and the city dump.

The thought of driving a taxicab seemed promising, although the hours were long. But if you hustled a lot of fares you could bring home a pretty decent paycheck with the tips and all. So I went down to the hack bureau ("hack" being the New York colloquialism for cabs and drivers) to fill out an application for a permit to drive a cab. However, when I started filling out the application a little voice said to me, "You don't really want to drive a cab, do you?" Actually, it was myself telling me I was foolish to drive a cab if my heart was not in it. Where there was no commitment there could not possibly be any fulfillment. Going to Food Trades had proven that. And with that philosophical thought helping me change my mind, I had run out of job options, not to mention money.

So I pulled out a thought I had been holding in abeyance —probably because I didn't want to consider it. I decided to call my half brother Buster, who was a handyman and had his own business. He, I figured, would be good for work a couple of days a week cutting lawns, painting houses, and various odd jobs. It would give me a few bucks, and in between I could continue my search for full-time employment, even reactivating past employment.

One such job I had had in 1958 was as a mutual funds salesman, which was a hot business during that time. I was, however, not your crackerjack mutual funds salesman. But now that I was having difficulty finding a suitable job, I began giving new consideration to selling mutual funds again. And I had also heard that Aetna Life Insurance Company was looking for applicants they could train and sponsor for the New York State insurance examination. So, with the idea of combining life insurance with mutual funds, I signed up for the training program at Aetna.

Meanwhile, I also advised Lee Myers at Collegiate of my job plight. Lee was my ace in the hole, since I had always maintained an excellent relationship with her and Mrs. Brown, and I felt that if push came to shove they would find me work when I had exhausted all other avenues. Sure enough, I got a

call a couple of days after I had spoken to Lee telling me about
an interview she had set up for me at the William Morris
Agency, a theatrical booking agency. Since I didn't know what
a theatrical booking agency was, I asked Lee. To my surprise,
and maybe that of many other people, I was told it was an employment agency for people in show business—actors, actresses,
directors, writers, singers, dancers, et cetera. It was hard to believe that all the performers I had seen on television, in the
movies, and performing in nightclubs used an employment
agency to get work. I had never thought of show business as
being work, or of show business people having jobs. That was
the illusion I and many others had as an outsider, which would
be clarified for me if I got the job at William Morris.

On another front, and the front-runner to what would be
instrumental in my own future, was the civil rights movement
going on in the 1960s. Actually, the movement had started in
the fifties with bus boycotts, sit-ins at lunch counters and public facilities in the southern states. And that was only the beginning. Later the civil rights movement attempted to raise the
consciousness of the major industries. Large corporations were
criticized because of their hiring practices when it came to
blacks. This was certainly true of theatrical agencies, and the
William Morris Agency, being one of the largest, was singled
out. The Morris Agency had one of the largest rosters of big-
name black entertainers, with Sammy Davis, Jr., the biggest.
But there were no black agents and never had been. So, when I
went on the interview, I knew I had at least one of the qual-
ifications for the job. I was definitely black.

I arrived for the interview at the William Morris Agency,
which at that time occupied several floors of 1750 Broadway,
armed to the teeth. I had with me my letter of reference from
Saks Fifth Avenue, a glowing recommendation from Lee Myers,
I was wearing my best suit and an attitude that said, "I am
the best man for the job." Fully realizing that first impressions
are lasting ones, I was determined to make a favorable and

lasting impression. I wanted to live up to the things that had been said about me by Lee Myers, who had told me that working for the William Morris Agency would have unlimited potential and opportunity. And, lastly, I really wanted (and needed) the job.

My interview was conducted by the personnel director, Bernard Leibowitz, and went great until he asked me if I had gone to college. Not only had I not gone to college, I had not graduated from high school in the normal manner. Therefore I made some tactical moves; I actuated a hard sell of myself. My accomplishments at Saks were first out of my mouth, plus the fact that Saks had seen fit to send me to NYU for special courses in retail merchandising. Naturally, I boasted about my education at Collegiate, and that I was a hard worker. In other words, I was asking for the opportunity to prove I could do the job. But despite all I had said, Mr. Leibowitz let me know they liked their trainees to be college graduates. He was also concerned I might be too old for their trainee program. I was twenty-four years old, and most of their trainees were twenty-one or twenty-two and just out of college.

Mr. Leibowitz liked me, though, and said I would have to meet with the comptroller, Sid Feinberg. That meeting took place a couple of days later, and I received his approval. It was decided by Mr. Feinberg that they would overlook my lack of a college degree since I had such high recommendations. To me, that proved one thing: it is possible to achieve what you want even when you fail to meet certain requirements and specifications. It's all a matter of gaining credibility through positive consistency and excellence.

But I wasn't out of the woods yet. There was one last person in this hierarchy "pecking order" who had to put his stamp of approval on my joining the William Morris Agency. This was Howard Hausman, one of the senior vice-presidents. Howard, however, was on a business trip to Europe. And, although I was assured the job was mine, nothing could be finalized until Howard returned. With that in mind, I decided to abandon all efforts to seek employment, although I did continue to prepare for the insurance examination. I figured that if by chance Howard did not concur with the others insurance and mutual funds would still be available for me to pursue. I felt you must have options.

However, the option which was literally my only source of income became a problem. Working with my half brother Buster was a now-and-then thing, with just about any day a workday. Since I was looking for a job this was usually okay—I would merely not look for work the day Buster wanted me to work. Well, Buster informed me that there was a particular Sunday he would need my help, but I told him I would not be available. I had promised my son Michael I would spend the day with him. And I always tried to keep the promises I made to Michael. When Sunday arrived Buster showed up at my house expecting me to go to work with him. I reminded him of what I had said previously, but that was unacceptable to Buster. Therefore a big dispute occurred which I did not want.

One of the reasons I always tried to avoid any kind of disagreement with Buster was because he was six feet, six inches tall, and he weighed quite a bit. He was strong, and I was fearful of his strength. The other disturbing part of our dispute was his accusation that Ruby, whom he called "Big Sister," loved me more than him, and that I didn't care about him either. This, I believe, was his reaction to being my half brother, which had nothing to do with how I felt about him, which at the moment was fear. Buster had been drinking prior to meeting me, and he was known to become violent when he was under the influence of alcohol. So I tried to reason with him, explaining and reexplaining what had been said by me, and that I could not break my promise. But all the time I was hoping he wouldn't hurt any of us. And he did not. But Buster did help me promise myself that if I got through this incident with him unharmed I would never be involved with him again. I didn't think it was worth the possibility of injury to try to get along with my half brother. That dispute took place in September, 1961, and for nineteen years we didn't speak to each other.

Anyway, while waiting to hear from William Morris, I passed the insurance exam, but I didn't have to use it. Howard Hausman returned from Europe, and I joined the William

Morris Agency. I was finally going to see if there was any truth to the saying, "There's no business like show business."

In 1961, when I joined William Morris, I was told I would not be given special treatment because I was black, and that I would be judged solely on the quality of my work and attitude. I thought that was more than fair, and I was prepared to take them at their word. Lee Myers was right. This was more than a job. It was a position with a golden opportunity, and the beginning of a career, although it began in the mailroom with a salary of fifty dollars per week. I returned to school on the GI Bill to supplement my income and also to sharpen my secretarial skills.

But that was okay. Some of the top agents in the company started in the mailroom. For instance, Irwin Winkler, who was in television packaging when I arrived and who later went on to produce such successful motion pictures as *They Shoot Horses, Don't They?* and each of the *Rocky* films, starring Sylvester Stallone. Also, a television agent named Bernie Brillstein who, when he left the Morris Agency, became a personal manager and developed an important client list that includes Jim Henson, creator of the Muppets, as well as Dan Aykroyd, formerly of the popular late night show, "Saturday Night Live," and now a film star too. Later, when I became a substitute secretary, I worked for both Irwin and Bernie. So, knowing that some of the top men in their fields had started in the mailroom, I was encouraged and felt that this was only a stepping-stone to my own eventual success in show business.

The mailroom was the ultimate test and the perfect training ground. We were the "boys" of the organization. "Can I have a *boy* to make a delivery to CBS?" "Can I have a *boy* to pick up some theater tickets at the Shubert Theater?" For me it was a new experience being called "boy" without the usual racial overtones accorded black men. Jim Hawkins, or "Uncle Jim" as we affectionately called him, was the dispatcher. He was in his seventies, and had been a writer for Fred Allen, who had been a show business pioneer in vaudeville and the early

days of radio. Uncle Jim was quite a character. He was a big
man, about six feet two, and heavy without being fat. His face
reminded me of a beagle's long jowls, rather puffy and aged.
He wore baggy clothes, which made you think he was still doing his vaudeville act, and he had a habit which I never got used
to. Uncle Jim would spit on the floor next to his desk. Everyone, including me, would look at this in amazement, but no
one would attempt to get him to stop spitting. Uncle Jim had a
mysterious power at the agency. We were never certain, but we
maintained he held some deep dark secrets about key people at
the Morris Agency.

In addition to our outside deliveries and pickups, our
mailroom duties included picking up and delivering interoffice
mail and sorting mail for delivery. Our duties also went as far
as the lavatories, where we had to refill soap and hand towel
dispensers and replace empty spools of toilet paper. And when
lunchtime arrived we would relieve receptionists and secretaries. As a matter of fact, it was while sitting in for a recep-
tionist that I saw Abe Lastfogel, the legendary chairman of
William Morris, who at that time was president, and who also
started in the mailroom. In show business circles Abe Lastfogel
is a most respected name. In William Morris circles it was a
name you responded to immediately.

It was moments like that—seeing Abe Lastfogel and knowing from whence he came—which also let me know that show
business was not all mail and toilet paper only. It was, I quickly
learned, a world where everybody wanted everything yesterday.
Working in the mailroom was a job that required you to listen,
be observant, have initiative, plenty of patience, and do what
you were told to do as quickly and efficiently as possible. It was
also the perfect place to be to see how the agency functioned;
you could literally see the business from the ground up. And
seeing and meeting all the personnel of the company allowed
me to draw my own conclusions and impressions of each one.

After several weeks I started to feel comfortable enough to
exert myself and to show some initiative. During my first three
weeks I noticed that the supplies and equipment, typewriters
and adding machines were desperately in need of some reor-

ganization. Saks had provided me with the expertise in this line of work, so I took it upon myself to clean and reorganize the entire area. Lou Metz, the supervisor of the mailroom, was so impressed that he turned the ordering and maintenance of the supplies over to me, which meant I would not have to make any outside deliveries or pickups. But there was another motive for what I had done. Once the area was organized it was easier for me to set up a typewriter during my lunch break. That way I could practice my typing, gain sufficient secretarial skills, and get myself sprung from the mailroom.

In less than two months my plan paid off. Between going to school at night and my typing practice during lunch, I acquired enough speed in typing and shorthand to be made a substitute secretary. And what a boost to my ego that was. But, more important, I received a boost in my pay—fifteen dollars per week. I was now making the grand total of sixty-five dollars per week. It was also a boost to my enthusiasm and excitement at working for the Morris Agency. My stay in the mailroom had been one of the shortest in the company's history.

Working as a substitute secretary was a great blessing and an extension of what I learned while working in the mailroom. Now I was exposed to the inner workings of all the various departments—motion pictures, literary, television, variety-nightclubs, concerts, legitimate theater, accounting, and legal. I also had the opportunity to develop relationships (some of which have lasted to this day) with many people at William Morris. Most of all, being a secretary brought me a step closer to my ultimate goal of becoming an agent. I had become very much hooked on show business, although I had only touched the fringes. But that was enough to let me know this was where I wanted to be.

Things were also working out well on the home front. I think the change in jobs—plus finally getting one I liked—was good for me. I was so busy trying to establish myself at William Morris, plus the long hours I was putting in at school, that I had little time for any outside affairs. Also, the birth of our second son, Gregory Wallace (I just had to get in the act), on February 7, 1962, brought Maria and me even closer. And I was once again blessed with the privilege of being involved with the miracle of birth. Of course I went through the same ritual at the hospital nursery that I performed when Michael was born—trying to get Gregory's attention with a lot of foolish faces and waving. Gregory didn't respond, naturally. And he still ignores me today when I make a fool of myself.

I do believe that, regardless of the number of children you have, each time is like the first time. There is an excitement and joy that is experienced with each new birth, which is unparalleled.

After several months as a substitute secretary I landed a permanent position with the person who had approved my employment at the William Morris Agency, Howard Hausman. By now Howard had become my mentor at the agency, and I had become one of his two secretaries. Actually, Howard was busy enough for three secretaries. But I later discovered that two were expected to do the work of three. Nevertheless, this promotion brought yet another salary increase—twenty-five dollars, I think—thus bringing my weekly pay to ninety dollars, five dollars more than when I had left Saks. Realizing this, I was not disappointed because it seemed as though I was starting all over. I felt that, from this point on, whatever I made would be more than I had before I came to the Morris Agency, and that I saw as progress.

Also, working with Howard was exciting and interesting because of his involvement in all phases of the agency, and it was on a very high level. I became an important secretary because I was working for one of the top executives. So now I was the secretary calling for a "boy" to run errands for me. It was a great ego massage.

The challenge for me while working for Howard was keeping up with him. On most days I was the first one in and the last one out of the office. At the end of the day I felt as if I had been chained to the typewriter. There were, of course, some benefits to all of this: my typing and shorthand skills improved to the point where I was better than most of those who had been at the agency longer than I. My self-confidence was also boosted, working with Howard. And not too long after, Howard became aware of the caliber of work I was doing, and he provided me the opportunity to exercise my own prerogative with his correspondence, as I deemed necessary. This confidence in my ability, plus working close with Howard, went beyond his being my mentor to his being like a father. He was always available to give me advice, and he would even loan me a few dollars when I found myself short (which was always) before payday.

Actually it was because of my obvious financial needs that Howard recommended I join the music department being formed. This was after I had spent five months working with him and feeling that if I was going to experience any progress in my career at the agency it would be because of Howard, and in another department I preferred. What I preferred might take months or even years, Howard explained to me like a father. Joining the music department would mean I was coming in at the beginning of a new department which had growth potential. I was still apprehensive, even though Howard was right. My problem was, I didn't like rock and roll music, and that was what the music department would be handling.

There were also my own evaluations of all the departments at the agency and my dream of being an agent one day in either the television or motion picture department. I soon realized what Howard was saying to me: it was a rather premature wish, and a case of naiveté, to think I would be assigned as an agent where I wanted to be. The music department was available and it had great potential, so go for it! And after a little more coaxing, plus a few more paydays of coming up short, I decided I had better try and develop a taste for rock and roll music.

One way of getting a job at William Morris without starting in the mailroom is to establish a name and reputation at another agency. That's how Rosalind Ross got to the William

Morris Agency and the supervision of the newly formed music department. Roz, as she was called, had been at G.A.C. (General Artists Corporation), and her name became synonymous with rock and roll. It helped that her roster of artists were top rock and roll acts like Fabian, Bobby Rydell, Dee Dee Sharp, Bobby Vee, Chubby Checker, Dion and the Belmonts, and many more. However, prior to Roz's arrival at William Morris, the feeling about rock and roll music was the same as mine; most agents in other departments considered it lowbrow and at the bottom of the entertainment ladder. Money, however, soon changed their minds.

This was after William Morris made a study and found that rock and roll was not a passing fad and could produce the same color money as their more reputable attractions. It was at that time William Morris decided to persuade Roz, her secretary, Esther, and one other agent, Jerry Brandt, to leave G.A.C. and bring their bag of tricks, and any of their roster of talent, to the William Morris Agency. Then I joined these new arrivals as Jerry's secretary, thus forming the nucleus for the first rock and roll music department at William Morris.

Working with Jerry Brandt provided an opportunity for me to gain both insight and experience in the day-to-day activity of an agent. I sat in on all the meetings, listened on the telephone when he made deals for clients, and did the paperwork necessary to issue a contract. Actually we issued a booking slip, which provided all the details necessary to the legal department so they could draw up a contract. In other words, being a booking agent is synonymous with being an employment agent. There was one other plus for me in working for Jerry: he didn't care for details or follow through, although he was a super agent. Therefore that became my responsibility, which I accepted very happily, as it put me closer to the trenches, so to speak, occupied by an agent.

And two and one half months after starting with the music department I found myself in the trenches as an assistant agent at the William Morris Agency. The fact that it did happen, and in less than one year, was due to Roz and Jerry, and my own aggressiveness while working in the music department. Roz and Jerry encouraged me to show all the initiative I could muster, and I went beyond the limit. This promotion also made my salary go beyond its previous limit, which I thanked Saks for. Their refusal of a raise forced me to seek my pot of gold down some other yellow brick road.

My becoming an agent meant I would be more deeply involved with show business, a business built solely on relationships with people. Most businesses are dependent upon people, but show business accentuates that fact more than any other business. There are people selling people, people buying people, people helping people, and people abusing people, ad infinitum.

Therefore, now that I was an agent, and the first black agent ever, at William Morris, I set some ground rules for myself—the principles by which I would always operate. First of all, I asked no performer to let me represent him or her solely on the basis of my being black. I wanted to represent clients who felt that I was qualified to secure them meaningful employment, and for a fee commensurate with their talent and popularity. And, in doing so, I would put forth my best efforts at all times to achieve those goals through whatever sources were available to me.

I decided that I would operate in an honest, open, and aboveboard manner, and that I would not patronize my associates or clients. In other words, there would be no ass kissing or lying by me. It was also my decision to build a reputation based on integrity, dignity, trust, ability, and hard work. Agents, I realized, had shady underhanded images, and I wanted to clearly establish that that was not the manner in which I operated.

So, with my new business cards confirming me as a duly authorized agent of the William Morris Agency, I set out to do just that.

6

I suppose I could have just settled for being the first black agent at a major theatrical agency and left it at that. After all, it was a major achievement in the show business world. But, considering what the opportunities had been prior to my break-through, the future didn't look that great for others to follow me. Therefore I was just about *it*. And with that responsibility I was very conscious of my obligation to become the best agent I could be.

One of the first things I had to do was clearly establish my identity and develop my own contacts in the show business community. It was a sure way to be the first to know about new talent. This did not mean that I was a talent scout. It was just that I had to always have a "willing" ear for the untried as well as the tried. I preferred to function that way, but it was not the norm of most agents. A few of my colleagues wanted to get their hands on someone they could book almost at the drop of someone's name. Not me. I sought the unpolished. And I usually found them through the people I knew in the business.

One of my earliest business relationships was with a tall, lanky, slow-talking black dude from Texas named Tom Wilson. He was also a Harvard graduate, very bright and quite witty, and one of the two token black record producers at Columbia Records. Tom and I hit it off immediately, probably because we had a lot in common. We both had a sense of humor, were ambitious, liked music, and had a strong interest in the opposite sex. And it was meeting and getting to know Tom that first brought me in contact with two new singers named Paul Simon and Art Garfunkel.

Tom, who was producing Simon and Garfunkel, had been telling me all about them and how fantastic and different they were. So one evening I decided to stop by their recording session to check them out. Well, the moment I saw and heard them I had to agree with Tom; Simon and Garfunkel were unique in every way, most noticeably so in their appearance. Paul was short and looked like Napoleon, while Art was taller with long blond hair that stood straight up on his head as though he had stuck his finger in a light socket. This hair also served to highlight Art's angelic face. But it was the blend of Paul's and Art's voices which was the pure magic and gave them an easily identifiable sound which I felt would bring great dividends once it was discovered. It was obvious that the foundation of that sound was in the lyrics Paul wrote, for he was a gifted songwriter who was able to transfer to song the concerns of the people.

Every agent longs to represent at least one big act. It is the one certain way to gain leverage and respect within the agency. And if that act is a big money earner, or has the potential to be one, then your worth as an agent, both monetarily and in prestige, increases. Since I saw in Simon and Garfunkel the unmistakable quality found in superstars, they were the first performers I brought into William Morris. Unfortunately, I was the only one at the agency who liked them. Most of my associates were more concerned with making fun of their name and Art's hair than considering their talent and potential. But I didn't let that deter me from what I believed, especially since Simon and Garfunkel recognized that my enthusiasm and respect for them were genuine.

I had hoped that once their album was completed all that I had felt would be confirmed. So when they released *Wednesday Morning, 3 A.M.*, the expectations were very high. Everyone at the record company was fired up over this first album for

Simon and Garfunkel. Several weeks after the album's release, however, nothing had happened and those expectations began to fade. When I heard the album I believed that every radio station in the country would play it, which was important for several reasons. Constant playing of their record on radio would generate album sales, thereby creating a demand for Simon and Garfunkel, which would enable me and my associates to secure engagements for them. At the same time, personal engagements would increase the demand for their album. This process is called the "snowball" effect in show business. However, I was wrong, and since the album didn't make it on the radio, I had to do something else.

I knew I had to generate interest at the agency, and so I had to find a way to get my associates in the music, television, and variety departments to see Simon and Garfunkel perform. That way, I was certain they would become as enthused as I was. I approached the Bitter End, a popular club in Greenwich Village where Bill Cosby, the Chad Mitchell Trio, and the Smothers Brothers had gotten started, but there was no interest. Eventually, I got them a couple of days at a club called Gerde's Folk City, also in Greenwich Village. This was not only good for showing them off to my associates at the agency, but it gave Simon and Garfunkel a chance to perform before a live audience. Most of their previous playing time had been at home, rehearsing, or in the recording studio. At any rate, when they appeared the reception was not overwhelming, and only a few people from Columbia Records and William Morris got by to see them perform. Since they didn't have a hit record, this was what I had to expect, and it seemed impossible for me to stimulate any interest at the agency.

About four or five months later, though, a report came in that a radio station in Miami, Florida, was getting good feedback on "Sounds of Silence," one of the selections from the album. This revived interest at Columbia Records, which had just about given up on Simon and Garfunkel, and Tom Wilson, who had just finished producing an album for Bob Dylan —the one that included "Like a Rolling Stone"—decided to go back into the studio and sweeten "Sounds of Silence" ("sweeten" is a media term for adding something extra to enhance a track or album, and to make it more commercial). The sweetened track was released, giving Simon and Garfunkel a new lease on their recording life, and it was soon clear that there was a hit record in Simon and Garfunkel's future.

Now that there was the potential of a hit record, I got a little more cooperation at the agency. We did book them some dates, although some people were still more into Art's hair than their music. I remember once sending Paul and Art a telegram at a date they were playing, telling them their record was on its way to being a definite hit and that under no circumstances should Art cut his hair.

By the time the departments in the agency got to work for Simon and Garfunkel they had changed managers and wanted to break their contract with William Morris. This was their right, because the contract promised a minimum amount of work within a certain time period, which promise had not been fulfilled by William Morris. So Simon and Garfunkel decided to go elsewhere. Suddenly everyone at the agency got into the picture to try to change their minds, but it was too late. They of course went on to become the superstars I always felt they were destined to be, both as a duo and individually. That was one of my first shots at a big act, and I lost, but I remained friends with Simon and Garfunkel and kept my integrity as an agent. They understood that I, personally, had believed in them from the start.

As I pointed out, I was a talent agent, not a talent scout. Therefore, any judgment made by me as to someone's talent was purely subjective. But it was also based on something I saw, or felt about a certain performer. During my period of growth as an agent, my instincts were alive quite often, just as they were when I first heard Simon and Garfunkel, with the results being a great education. That education, however, must not have sunk in completely when I came across a singer named Nancy Wilson, because I was still scouring for that "big" act.

Nancy, who I had had my eye on for a long time, was a jazz singer who was causing a lot of people to sit up and take notice. And I was one of them. So, when I heard that Nancy was being released from her contract at MCA, the largest booking agency at the time, I saw it as another opportunity to bring an act into the agency that would be good for the agency, and good for me.

Because I thought Nancy had great potential, I contacted her manager, a gentleman named John Levy, who had an impressive client list of musical talent. When I met with John I was completely taken by surprise because he had skin that was as black as mine. Somehow I just knew, or assumed, that he would be Jewish, and, of course, white. But, as always, life is full of lessons. As sure as you cannot judge a book by its cover, you also cannot tell a Levy by his name.

After I recovered, John and I hit it off immediately, mainly because he was so straightforward and showed evidence that he knew his way around show business. I felt comfortable talking with him. He accepted my pitch that William Morris could do a good job in guiding Nancy Wilson's career, which was still developing. We both agreed, however, that some of the key people at the agency should see Nancy perform, and if they were as enthusiastic as I was, then our talks would go further.

Since Nancy's first engagement in the New York City area would be one week at the Apollo Theater in Harlem, that would be my target location. I immediately began campaigning by sending recordings, photographs, and a biography to my associates at William Morris, along with an invitation to the Apollo. Most of the agents were afraid to go to Harlem, because it was almost exclusively populated with black people and could be rough. However, I was able to get some of the agents to venture uptown to catch the show. One of the agents thought she was just another jazz singer, while another, who was noted for molding and guiding careers, thought she should dress differently. What that agent didn't realize was that Nancy was pregnant with her first child. But, comments aside, the marriage of Nancy Wilson and William Morris never came off, and the agency lost a brilliant talent who went on to have an illustrious career. My gain was in meeting and remaining friends with Nancy as well as John Levy, both of whom would be beneficial for me in my future show business dealings and career.

When I was not looking for my "big act," I was servicing the ones we represented, such as Solomon Burke, an incredibly charming R&B (rhythm and blues) singer who had a habit of calling me from all over the country to ask that I advance him money, and singer Sam Cooke, whom I traveled with on his tour. Traveling with an R&B tour was like being at a party, and traveling with Sam Cooke was like being with the host of the party. "Having a Party" was not only one of Sam's biggest hit records, it was something he loved to do, frequently, and was just one of the things I liked about being exposed to this great performer and the people around him.

I first met Sam Cooke in 1963 in Norfolk, Virginia, at the beginning of a tour of one-nighters of black acts which Sam headlined and which included Dionne Warwick and Lloyd Price. Right after I checked into the Holiday Inn I went over to the rehearsal at the auditorium. One of the stipulations in Sam's contract was that his backup band, the Upsetters, would also work for the other acts, which was good for Sam but not the best idea for the other acts. Since the Upsetters could not read music, they had to listen to the other performers' records to learn the material, and their ears were not always as well tuned as their instruments.

Dionne Warwick, who was making her first appearance on a tour as a result of her first hit single, "Don't Make Me Over," found out how true to their names the Upsetters were when they played for her. During rehearsals Dionne listened to the band butcher her songs so badly that it made the young singer almost cry. There was nothing she could do except keep trying until they got it right. Well, that night when Dionne went on, the Upsetters were no better, but Dionne—the champion performer she was then and still is—rose to the occasion and was able to bring the house down, in spite of being personally upset by the Upsetters.

As for Sam Cooke's performance, the Upsetters had his music down perfect, but Sam could create his own magic when he performed. He had what we know today as charisma. He didn't jump all over the stage or rip off his clothing to arouse an audience. He stayed in one position, tapping his feet and offering a few sexy inflections and expressions which would drive the ladies mad with passion and make the men in the audience envious but never jealous—just wishing they had the same talent with which to capture a woman.

Seeing this night after night left me awestruck and excited. And with Sam Cooke being such a big important star in every city he toured, I became an important agent to the entertainment people in each of those cities. This was particularly good for me because I was still somewhat reserved and liked to keep a low profile. While I sometimes could not avoid appearing to be the big-time agent, underneath that facade was a frightened neophyte who still had a lot of maturing to do.

Being with Sam and sharing his limousine helped me to overcome my lack of regard for myself. Once I was accepted as a part of the show, and not just some eavesdropper from the agency, I found myself doing much more than I was required to do for Sam Cooke. For instance, there was the time I was called upon to drive Sam's limousine. I was probably one of the only agents to have chauffeured a client, which was *really* servicing a client beyond the call of duty.

I left the tour before it was completed to return to New York, and carried with me a great education, a much improved self-image, and the fact that Sam Cooke and I had developed a warm personal relationship. This continued, and when he was in New York he often had dinner with me and my family. Also, I had always admired a gold pinky ring he wore, and one day I received in the mail a ring to match his. I thought that was very generous of him, and it definitely sealed our friendship for life. And when his life was taken from us all, I felt a deep personal loss. But I also felt good because I had been given the opportunity to know and become friends with this richly talented human being who touched me in a positive way. Each time I look at my pinky, and the ring Sam gave me, I smile, and even laugh, because of the happy memories Sam Cooke gave me—and so many others—to have forever. Thanks, Cooke.

If touring with Sam Cooke was a traveling party, with Sam as the host, then touring with Dick Clark was a school outing, and Dick Clark was the headmaster. One thing I found out, the two touring groups were as different as night and day, and literally so. Dick's tours were never less than seventy-five percent white, with stars of the time like Bobby Rydell, Bobby Vee, and Gene Pitney.

They were all part of the tour package Dick Clark owned and headlined, which meant he also guaranteed the performers' salaries. We at the William Morris Agency, as Dick Clark's representatives, would buy all the acts and then sell the show as well, with most tours about three or four weeks. Because of Dick's very popular "American Bandstand," it was easy to buy the acts and easy to sell the show, particularly since the radio stations sponsored the dates. Teenagers all over the country loved Dick's show and longed to see him as much as the acts he was presenting. My job was to serve him and his acts in much the same way I had worked with Solomon Burke and Sam Cooke, but it turned out to be much different because of the personalities of each of the tours and their headliners.

There was one particular date on Dick's tour, in Winston-Salem, North Carolina, that ran into some difficulties because it was integrated. It seemed the local Ku Klux Klan chapter didn't care how much their children loved Dick Clark's "American Bandstand" on television, they didn't want him attempting to mix the races in their city. This, of course, had Dick very concerned—along with yours truly—and he hired extra security as a precaution. The only problem with this wise move on Dick's part was that you could never be sure they were not also Klan members. But in the end the show came off without a hitch until Dick's party for the performers after the concert, when word began to circulate that the Klan were on their way. We decided not to test the rumor, and Dick personally engineered our evacuation from the building and into the bus faster than any fire drill I had ever participated in when I was in school. That was just one of the many nice things about Dick Clark: always the good headmaster, and always showing the proper concern for his students. Interestingly enough, this

particular troubled booking was handled by me. I should have
been suspicious of something when the promoter and I first
met, and he gave me a double take. Up until that time our
deals had been via telephone, so he must have assumed I was
white. This was reminiscent of the first time I met John Levy,
who I had assumed was Jewish when he was really black. And
therein was one more valuable lesson: never assume anything!

A Dick Clark tour during the summer of 1964 is particularly memorable because I booked three beautiful girls named
Florence Ballard, Mary Wilson, and Diana Ross, who were a
singing group called the Supremes. This was their first major
engagement, but they soon became the most popular and well-
known female singing group of all time. I might not have
booked them if it hadn't been for the persistence of Motown
Records, who wanted William Morris to take them on even
though we were not really interested.

Actually, we were interested in representing Mary Wells,
who was one of Motown's hottest attractions at the time because of such hits as "My Guy" and "You Beat Me to the
Punch." She was perfect to the William Morris way of thinking: sustained bookings were just about guaranteed if the artist had records getting a lot of air play. So naturally we wanted
Mary Wells, but Motown would not let us have her if we didn't
take this relatively new, and still unknown, group called the Supremes, which I had heard of at the beginning of 1964. Esther
Edwards, the sister of Berry Gordy, Jr., the founder and guiding hand of Motown Records, had told me all about the Supremes, but I was not interested. And I knew that William
Morris would not be interested either. But we did want to
develop a long-term relationship with Motown since the evidence was already there that they were going to be around a
long time. Getting Motown would have been a major feather
in my agent's cap.

But it was not going to be easy. Esther Edwards was firm
in her desire to push the Supremes, and William Morris was
locked into their policy about artists having a record getting air
play before booking them. Therefore we were never able to
come to terms for Mary Wells, although I kept the lines of

communication open to Motown. Then after a couple of months Motown had another hit act in singer Brenda Holloway, whose record, "Every Little Bit Hurts," had gone to the top of the charts. Brenda, a beautiful black girl from Los Angeles, could sing for days. And we at William Morris decided she would be perfect on a Dick Clark tour we were putting together for the summer of 1964. Going to Motown with an offer to put Brenda with Dick Clark was a natural—including five hundred dollars per week with a certain number of days guaranteed—but not to Esther Edwards, as it turned out.

Call it stubbornness or dedication, but Esther and Motown had not given up on the Supremes. If we wanted Brenda we had to take the Supremes. This time, though, they let us listen to a new record by the Supremes which they were high on, and once we listened to the test pressing we agreed to take a chance with them. The price for Brenda remained the same, and we got the Supremes (all three) for six hundred dollars per week, which was a low price. Had their record been out, they would have cost more. Motown knew, though, that these tours were not done for money but to promote records. And that test pressing of the Supremes' "Where Did Our Love Go?" became a number one record shortly after they finished the tour. The lesson of Motown's commitment and dedication to their artists was one that would help me in my own career.

My recollection of these three young singers known as the Supremes—Diana Ross, Mary Wilson, Florence Ballard—is one of honesty and innocence, which was the image Motown wanted to keep intact. That's why they had a road manager, Don Foster, and Diana's mother acting as a chaperon. But, as fledgling singers trying to get started, they were like any other hopefuls: they complained constantly that they would never have a hit record. And since most of the other acts on Motown had one or more hits already, the Supremes felt they were too far behind to catch up. I had to agree with them, especially when looking at their stage wardrobe of gold and silver lamé shoes with holes in them, and their colorless dresses. But these three determined and talented teenage singers would not be denied. They were obviously destined for superstardom, and superstars the Supremes became. And I was there looking on at history in the making.

I wasn't around in 1775 when Paul Revere made his famous midnight ride to warn the community, "The Redcoats are coming! The Redcoats are coming!" But I was around in 1964 when the Beatles invaded our American shores with their music and became the forerunners of many other English bands seeking to change America's musical taste. The English made such an impression that American acts at that time found it difficult to get air play and decent bookings. So a cockney tongue became a license to steal, almost.

At the William Morris Agency we were as interested in the English invasion as anyone and got our share of British bands to sell. Our worldwide offices, plus our own Monday morning reading of the music trades—*Billboard, Cashbox,* and *Record World*—kept us way ahead of everyone else. That's why we were the first to handle the Rolling Stones, the second most popular group to come from England. Jerry Brandt's signing of the Rolling Stones was unique for the William Morris Agency, since they were a very establishment company—something the Rolling Stones show the most disdain for. But money can change the color of a lot of points of view. However, it was *my* color which led me to become friends with Eric Burdon, the lead singer with another popular English act called the Animals.

When the Animals made their first American appearance at the Paramount Theater in Times Square, I went by to visit them as a representative of William Morris. When I met Eric, the first thing he wanted to know was if I would take him to the Apollo Theater in Harlem. This was important to Eric because he had spent years reading, researching, and collecting materials on black people in all walks of life, with black musicians and their music a particular specialty. Therefore being in New York City near the Apollo was too good to be true. And meeting me was more than he could have wished for, since not too many of my agency colleagues would dare set foot in Harlem if they didn't have to.

The visit to this legendary theater was like going to Mecca for Eric, who was in a semitrance as he viewed the large photographs in the lobby of Billie Holiday, Duke Ellington, Nat "King" Cole, Harry Belafonte, and many great black performers who had made the Apollo great. I felt something special bringing Eric to the Apollo, and especially watching someone outside of my black world appreciate the artists and music I had more or less taken for granted as the best in the world. Eric appreciated my bringing him to this historical landmark, and I appreciated Eric Burdon for helping me remember how rich my own heritage really is.

My overzealous desire to succeed as an agent had led me to neglect other, more personal areas, namely, my family. I rationalized this neglect as having to do with the fact that my two years as an agent had been the most hectic years of my life. So, if I had to attend a different nightclub each night, or concerts on the weekend, or recording sessions whenever, it was all for the purpose of furthering my career as an agent, which would in turn help my family's future. Of course Maria thought I should have invited her along for some of this socializing in show business circles. I disagreed for two reasons; seeing myself as a playboy meant seeing what I could find on those evenings, and our sons, Michael and Gregory, who were four and two, needed their mother at home with them.

More important, though, was the fact that I had never totally committed myself to married life. The only time I spent at home was Saturday and Sunday. I had a terrific desire to succeed, so I worked very hard. But I also convinced myself that I was unhappy at home and that marriage was no longer for me, so the job helped me stay away from home. I also wanted the glitter and trappings that so frequently go with show business, so I began to indulge in extramarital relationships. And when you play with fire you usually get burned.

One day I opened a package of shirts just back from the local Chinese laundry and found that the top shirt was cut to ribbons. I was particularly disturbed by this since it was one of my favorite dress shirts and was the last piece of clothing I had

bought while in Hawaii, so when I saw it ruined I confronted
the owner of the laundry. He said that was the condition of the
shirt when it came in. And with a little closer examination of
the shirt, I noticed lipstick stains on the collar. It was now obvious to me what had happened: Maria had also seen the lipstick stains and had taken her anger out on my shirt. For me,
that was a definite warning that I had better hang my clothes
elsewhere. No telling, the next time I might be *in* the shirt
that was cut to ribbons.

True, I did have a choice: clean up my act or leave. I
chose the easier of the two by leaving. During that period of
my life I always took the easy way out. But leaving this time
was twice as painful as the first, since I was leaving two sons instead of just one. And just like the first time, I did not know
how to explain to my young sons why Maria and I would no
longer be living together. It was one of those situations, I later
decided, that had to be turned over to God and allowed to take
its natural course. I had spent a major portion of that marriage
wishing I were single; now I had my wish.

My new bachelorhood meant I needed someplace to live,
which I found with a friend of mine and a client I had signed
at William Morris, named Johnny Thunder. He had been a
lead singer with one of the Ink Spots groups, of which there
had been several. In 1963, Johnny had a hit record entitled
"Loop de Loop." Johnny's apartment was perfect, and I was
glad to get settled. But that first week of being single was not
to be believed. It was as if I had been stranded on a lonely island for years without seeing women. I pursued every female
who crossed my path, almost as if it were my duty to. But that
pace didn't last long, not after I realized how expensive it was
to support two households. Also, I may have left my family,
but I was still committed to their welfare, and that was more
important to me than being able to be a big spender.

I was also pleased that Maria and I were able to work out
what was best for her and the boys' welfare with a lawyer without going to court. I did not resent having to pay child support
and alimony; I clearly saw that as my responsibility. Maria also
put no restrictions on when I could see Michael and Gregory,

because she knew how I felt about them. And as for any differences Maria and I had, they were never allowed to interfere with the relationship each of us had with our two sons.

It's amazing what time and personal growth through life experiences can do to change one's viewpoint and character. As I write about my early experiences and growth, I sometimes feel as though I am writing about another human being in another lifetime. The values that I have today would never allow me to behave as I did then. That to me is one of the great redeeming aspects of life: you have the opportunity daily to outgrow your past mistakes. Each day is, literally, a brand-new beginning. And as Eric Butterworth, the minister of the Unity Center of Practical Christianity in New York City, says, "The object is not to go through life but to grow through life."

7

"*Failure will never overtake you if your
determination to succeed is strong
enough.*"

—JESS LAIR

From 1964 to 1966 the life I led after separating from Maria
ran a regular course. First of all, there were my relationships
with the opposite sex, in which the chase was always more exciting than the actual catch. The thrill of the romance was
what held my attention, and I had developed a style that
proved rather successful. I would send flowers and thoughtful
cards, and occasionally pick up a date in a limousine. And it
was always impressive to attend a television show or nightclub
and be able to visit the dressing room backstage and introduce
my date to the star. That was my playboy-bachelor approach,
which went on for almost two years, and which I got tired of.

It got so that nothing had any meaning after the catch. As
soon as I went to bed with a girl the romance was over. I was
just never willing to make a commitment because I could never
see beyond the game of pursue and conquer. There were, however, some girls I considered making a go of it with, but they
were not interested in long-term relationships. So my single life
was not as satisfying as I had imagined it would be. I also
found out once again that the grass is *not* necessarily greener
on the other side. Therefore I made a slight retreat to what I

truly loved and was committed to, my sons Michael and
Gregory.

By now I had gotten my own apartment—a one-bedroom
with a balcony, located on Central Park West. The only furniture I had was a bed which I had purchased new, and a used
couch I bought from one of my associates at William Morris.
In addition I had a television set, and the stove and refrigerator
came with the apartment. So, even with the sparseness of furnishings, I was happy to finally have my own place, someplace
I could bring Michael and Gregory. Sharing an apartment was
okay, but it was not private. Now if I wanted to be loud and
have a good time with my sons when they came, I didn't dis-
turb anyone. Also I got a great kick out of cooking for my two
boys, although they had to settle for a lot of pancakes and
french toast, which were my specialties, thanks to my Food
Trades/Essex House training.

However, just about the time I had relaxed my playboy
way of life and settled in to be entertained more by my sons, I
met a beautiful and shapely lady from Raleigh, North Carolina, named Shirlee Ellis. Her stage name was Shirlee May, and
she was a singer. An associate in the publicity department at
William Morris asked me if I would meet with Shirlee to see if
I could help her get some work. Since I had seen her photographs, when I said okay I wasn't sure I could get her work, but
I was positive I wanted to meet her.

When we met at my office we talked for over an hour
about everything except getting her work. Then, when she was
leaving, I asked her to have dinner with me. She looked
stunned and, like the proper southern lady she was, she replied,
"But I don't know you." And that shocked me. However, I
continued to make my plea, maybe almost to the point of beg-
ging, but she never replied, and thanked me for seeing her.
That turnoff of me became my turnon for her.

But it was not the usual thing I felt when I pursued a
woman in order to conquer her. I began to see Shirlee as *the*
girl I had been waiting for: the person who could change my
life. I therefore felt it was more than a challenge to get a date
with her; it was of the utmost necessity. I tried several times

with no luck. And it was not until a month after our first meeting, and a barrage of telephone calls, flowers, cute little cards, and whatever charm I could muster, that she finally agreed to see me. Shirlee probably figured that would be the one way to get rid of me. Well, if that was her reason, it backfired, because after that meeting we began seeing each other regularly.

But there was another obstacle between us: her singing career. Shirlee had to work during July and August 1966 in Atlantic City, New Jersey, at the Club Harlem, a very famous nightclub of those days. Shirlee and I had a telephone relationship on weekdays, and on Fridays after work I would rent a car and drive to Atlantic City to be closer to her. These trips could not be too frequent, because I was still committed to my sons, and so devoted some of my time to them.

There was also my concern about how my sons and Shirlee would get along. This became important to me as I saw my relationship with Shirlee growing. I knew how I felt about her, and I wanted her to meet Gregory and Michael, which was also my unconscious way of getting an okay of sorts to think seriously about her. Well, Shirlee and my sons hit it off great, and that gave me the green light to proceed with whatever I foresaw as our future together.

All during the summer and into the fall Shirlee and I remained romantically linked. Then, one September evening while strolling through Central Park, I asked her to marry me. By doing so, I decided to put behind me my playboy, unsettled days, which was a big step for me. And on Friday, October 21, 1966, we were married at the Broadway United Church of Christ in New York City. Again, my reception was a small one, at the Russian Tea Room near Carnegie Hall, accompanied by my best man, Chuck Fly, and Shirlee's maid of honor, Adrienne Kennedy. Also, like my first marriage, there was no honeymoon, since I could not take the time off. All we could afford was a weekend, which was spent at the cute and cozy Stonehenge Inn in Connecticut. There we both experienced the spectacular beauty of nature as the seasons changed, and we began our new life together—which this time I vowed would be different.

Around January of 1967 I began to get restless at William Morris. I had been booking rock and roll acts since 1962 and I was beginning to feel burned out. Also the music was changing. We had entered the hard rock, or acid and psychedelic rock, phase of music, and I was having difficulty relating to the loudness. This was the era of Jefferson Airplane, the Grateful Dead, Canned Heat, and the legendary Jimi Hendrix, a period that will probably be remembered as the most self-destructive in musical history, because performers were killing themselves through excessive use of drugs and alcohol.

The musical emphasis had shifted from quality and meaningful lyrics to cacophonous amplification, and from entertainment to exhibition. Showmanship was now a lost art. I could not then, and I cannot today, relate to guitars and musical instruments being destroyed on stage in the name of entertainment. I know all about the millions of people who paid millions of dollars to encourage and make millionaires of these exhibitionists, but that only proves that we all have different tastes. Also, I'm not judging or criticizing the music, the musicians, or the people who supported it. I am simply giving my opinion, which was part of my reason for ultimately making the decision I did. Furthermore, I was beginning to feel stagnant, and it was becoming a chore for me to go to work. I suppose I was spoiled by my rapid growth during the first years at the agency and so was especially disappointed that my growth was now being stunted.

Prior to these moments of reflection, there were some changes in the music department at William Morris, including a few changes at the helm. Roz had left in 1965 to join Dick Clark's company, and Jerry Brandt moved in as the department head. I then became second in seniority. There were two other agents—Larry Kurzon and Harvey Kresky—and two agents in the college division—Jay Jacobs and Steve Leber. Under Jerry's direction the revenue of the department continued to increase, but the department became fragmented and morale began to sink. We lost the cohesiveness we had had as a group when Roz was in charge. This was partially because Jerry was a great deal maker but didn't have the patience to follow through and give direction.

Then in 1966 Jerry left William Morris to become a partner in a nightclub in Greenwich Village called the Electric Circus. With Jerry's departure my elevation to department head seemed inevitable. First of all, I was the senior member in the department. And during all my years at the agency I had been reliable and responsible, and I had an excellent reputation throughout the industry. I also had supervisory experience, which I had gotten at Saks Fifth Avenue. So, in my opinion, I had everything the job required. Well, that's not what the management at William Morris thought.

I did not get the position because it was felt that the other agents would not take direction from me because I was black. (There was only one other minority member in the department, a Puerto Rican named Hector Morales, who was my secretary. Hell, I found that hard to believe, simply because I had helped train some of the agents and had watched them work their way up. At any rate, this was my first indication, since joining William Morris in 1961, that my future there was limited. And that's when I became restless. Once I learned that Steve Leber would be the new music department head, my interest in remaining with that department plummeted. I began thinking about a transfer to the television or motion picture department, which is where I had originally wanted to go before I was talked into joining the new music department. It was Howard Hausman who had said I would have a better chance to grow there and he had been right. And it was Howard who was now telling me that the television and motion picture departments would also be out of my reach because of the color of my skin.

It seemed the ever mysterious *they* felt the television networks and motion picture studios were not ready to accept a black agent. What *they* didn't know was that *we* are not ready to accept ninety-nine percent of life that comes our way. And *they* will never be ready unless someone tells them when to be ready. Most of us are afraid to be ready because being ready means accepting *change*, and you know how we fear change.

What a distressing paradox I had become entwined in. Here I was hired because I was black, and now I could not advance because I was black. Talk about a Catch-22 situation!

After all of those letdowns, my interest in William Morris went into a semicoma. That didn't mean I stopped doing my job. Oh no, I was too filled with initiative to do anything that would destroy all that I had accomplished up to that point. What I did was find another challenge while I attempted to sort out my future. Fortunately for me, that challenge turned out to be a black South African trumpet player named Hugh Masakela whom I had recently signed to the agency. Once again, it was my friend Tom Wilson who introduced me to Masakela while he was recording the trumpeter for MGM Records. Right away I saw that there was something rare and different about Masakela. Although his music was jazz-oriented, there was the happy, infectious "high life" sound which made it more commercial. There was something here for me to work with, and we all agreed we wanted to make the African sound happen.

One of the major challenges we would have to overcome in order to make that happen was to find a means of survival. Nobody in Masakela's group had any income, and the small advance Masakela had from the record company was long since gone. I therefore went to William Morris to ask them for a $1,250 loan for Masakela. This was not easy, especially since they were not holding any deposits on future dates—nor were any future dates planned—for Masakela. But I went to Howard Hausman and asked him to help me get the loan, and he did. The reason he did it was because of my enthusiasm for Masakela and my proven ability to spot and develop talent. Masakela certainly was a talent, which was why I spent so much time with his career. It was somewhat of a juggling act dealing with Masakela, trying to stay stimulated enough to handle my other responsibilities at the agency, and trying to spend some time with my new bride.

I had not yet learned of the concept of husband and wife discussing things together, especially things that could affect our home, like leaving my job. That had been one of my prob-

lems when I was with Maria. I had always lived with the belief
that the husband worked those things out and the wife was informed of the decision. It was my responsibility to provide, I
thought, and my wife should not be bothered by such things.
That feeling was quite chauvinistic of me, but at that space and
time that was my level of consciousness.

The weeks of working with Masakela eventually got me to
look squarely at everything happening to me. I looked at my
lack of interest in rock and roll music, my being passed over for
music department head, and my not being able to transfer to
another department, and I decided to take leave of the William Morris Agency. In many ways it was very similar to my situation at Saks Fifth Avenue. I felt I had gone as far as I could
go, and I wanted to do more with my life than book rock and
roll acts. I didn't feel my decision to leave William Morris was
wrong, but I do feel it was wrong of me not to discuss my decision to leave with Shirlee.

Once I gave my two-week notice I felt relief, and there was
none of the unpreparedness that I had felt when I left Saks.
During my six and one half years at William Morris I had
gained a wealth of knowledge and made many important personal contacts. In show business, contacts play an important
role in where you can go and how far. Sometimes they are more
important than talent. I left the agency with the feeling that I
had what I needed to promote Masakela well, and that I would
make him a superstar. I also had a master plan: I was going to
build a self-contained, musically oriented entertainment company handling recording, music publishing, and personal management, and Masakela would be the lead act. Working with
Masakela in the recording end of the business would be a longtime friend of his named Stewart Levine, and working with
me, handling personal management and appearances, public
relations and promotion, would be a very good friend of mine
named Chuck Fly, whose standard greeting was: "Chuck Fly,
wonderful guy," which he was and continues to be.

My first project with Masakela was a concert at Philharmonic Hall (since changed to Avery Fisher Hall) in the Lincoln Center complex in New York City. This was our way of launching Hugh Masakela in a big way, because the feeling was then and still is that any major success in the Big Apple is heard all over the world. Another reason for playing Lincoln Center was Gary Keyes, the promoter, who had promoted some very successful and stylish concerts at this same location. All we needed was money, which I provided.

This was money I had borrowed from the bank, plus the pension share I received when I left William Morris. Gary Keyes warned me that it was risky spending my own money since most of Masakela's following were underground people. He was considered a word-of-mouth act that was happening at the moment; there were no guarantees Masakela would still be happening at the time of the concert. We looked at the concert as a career move rather than a profit-making venture, although we certainly wouldn't refuse any profits received. So, in my opinion, spending the money was an investment in the future, although I did not consult Shirlee about it.

The day of the concert arrived quickly, but the advance sales were slow. We were, however, still optimistic that the people would turn out en masse to experience what we felt would be an exceptional evening of entertainment. Well, it takes more than optimism. Not only did the people not turn out en masse, there were not even enough people there to make my investment back. As a result, I lost over three thousand dollars, a fact which was not overlooked by Shirlee. Nevertheless, I remained the eternal optimist and looked at the brighter side: favorable press notices and an energetic response from those who had come to the concert. I also decided I could not cry over these losses and that I should press on because I believed in the success of Masakela. That belief was encouraged when, because of the concert, Masakela received an invitation to appear at the First Monterey Pop Festival, which was being held in Monterey, California, during June 1967. This was a major appearance for Masakela, who was joining such recording stars as Jimi Hendrix, Canned Heat, Janis Joplin, the Mamas and the Papas, and many more. Even though he was not as well known as the rest of the bill, Masakela held his own and was a big success, which I hoped would mean dollars soon, since Shirlee was now pregnant.

By the time it was discovered Shirlee was with child, she was five months gone, and neither she nor I realized it. She had gotten sick several times but never connected it with being pregnant. And we couldn't tell by her menstrual cycle because it was always irregular. Well, when we visited the doctor the pregnancy was confirmed. We were surprised because we had figured, and even planned, not to have any children for a couple of years, which meant we didn't plan too well, even with the help of the Pill. But whether the news was expected or not, we both looked forward to and prepared for that blessed event.

To make back the money I'd invested, I intensified my efforts to secure work for Masakela. I was also helping Chuck Fly promote our first single release, "Chisa," which we produced and distributed through UNI Records, a company that had been recently formed by MCA, Inc. Masakela was their first and only artist at the time. In addition to trying to get the record played, I was the personal manager and agent, as well as the road manager. This meant I went on the road a lot to check on the bookings and to see that the sound and the lights at a club were right, pay the hotel bill, collect the fee for the date, and coordinate radio and newspaper interviews. When I wasn't chasing down those necessities, I was out chasing the girls in the different cities I visited. True, I was still married, but that didn't stop this need—or maybe I thought it was my duty—to bed the opposite sex. I also may have just been trying to impress everyone with my ability to attract women.

Cheating on my wife meant lying to her as well, which I did many times. On one occasion when Masakela was playing in Washington, D.C., I made plans to leave New York on Sunday for a date that was starting on Tuesday. Ordinarily, I would have gone on the Monday, but I decided to leave early so I could hook up with a girl I had met on a previous trip there. Shirlee became enraged since it seemed that I didn't care about her being pregnant and didn't want to spend any time with her. It was not that; I just wanted to have my cake and eat it too, as the saying goes.

There were many times in my relationships with Shirlee and Maria when I just had to have my own way, even at the expense of damaging their feelings. It's too bad that I was not at the level of consciousness I am today. Had I been, I would have been more loving and supportive, instead of greedy, deceitful, and devious, all of which derive from fear and an absence of inner peace. What I had not yet come to grips with was knowing, loving, and accepting myself. Therefore it was impossible to love anyone else.

Despite my obvious shortcomings, Shirlee and I continued to make our lives work. This was helped by the fact that she had a new life existing within her, with a birth date scheduled for sometime in September 1967. Also, a decision had been reached to move the entire Masakela team, with the exception of Chuck Fly, to Los Angeles, which I agreed to do after Shirlee gave birth. It was a good business move since our record deal was with UNI Records, located in Los Angeles, and Masakela's business manager, Larry Spector, was situated there. My only regret in making the move was that I would not be able to see Michael and Gregory regularly, and leaving Ruby. However, since Ruby and I were not getting along that well, being miles apart might help our relationship. This would be a good test to see if absence *really* makes the heart grow fonder.

As the doctor had predicted, Shirlee gave birth to a bouncing baby boy, who we thought was going to be a girl, on September 13, 1967. We named him Shawn Ellis, a name with a history behind it. Since Shirlee's father was named John, we used the Irish version of John, and Shirlee's maiden name, Ellis, became his middle name. It was a very happy moment, and I was especially overjoyed about having three sons. Our joy, however, was slightly shaded when we learned that Shawn had yellow jaundice and would require a complete blood replacement. Both Shirlee and I were very concerned about our baby, but the doctor allayed our fears when he explained there was no danger and that the transfusion was routine. So when Shirlee came home it was without Shawn, who had to remain in the hospital an extra week.

Once the week was up we had Shawn home with us. But Shirlee, unlike most new mothers, did not spend the first month getting to know her baby and recuperating from childbirth. She spent her time packing boxes and coordinating our arrangements to move to Los Angeles. I also chipped in, and because of my prior experience I was able to help by changing diapers, making formula, and bathing Shawn. The moving plan was that I would accompany Shirlee and Shawn to Raleigh, where she would stay with her mother and sister Barbara for one month. I would continue on to Los Angeles and get things in order for their eventual arrival. When the date of departure arrived, Chuck Fly, who would continue to coordinate Masakela's activities on the East Coast, drove us to the airport, and we headed for California, as so many had before, with high hopes of making our fortune.

Los Angeles provided for me a whole new feeling of enthusiasm. This was where the action was: our record company, television shows, and that aura which Hollywood is so well known for. A house in the Hollywood Hills was rented by Masakela and Stu Levine, which would double as my office and living quarters. It was perfect, with two bedrooms and a nice little backyard—quite a change from apartment living in New York. I looked forward to Shirlee and Shawn joining me and sharing what I knew was going to be a happy home and life. Until that time I kept busy getting things organized, making new contacts and renewing old ones. The time passed quickly, and before I knew it I had Shirlee and Shawn with me. With all that was happening I was on a special high.

But it didn't last long. I had retained that inability to be flexible, which showed its inconsiderate self sometime after we had gotten settled. At first we'd gone out, made friends, and tried to enjoy our new life together. We also joined the United Church of Christ, which was recommended by our pastor in New York. Church was something I had not done in a long time, and when I did, it was in New York, and because of

Shirlee. Other than a few friends and church, we spent most of our time at home. My time there was usually spent handling Masakela's career and having meetings with various people.

Many times when Shirlee and I were alone together, I would not talk to her. My mind was always on the business, plus I harbored a lot of hang-ups that made it impossible for me to try to hold a meaningful conversation with Shirlee. For that reason she would plead with me to talk to her, saying that she needed to talk to someone other than Shawn. It was almost as if she was pleading to deaf ears, since I continued to offer her no support. Eventually the stress and tension of it all—moving, having a baby, trying to find a sounding board and support and companionship—got to Shirlee and she had to be hospitalized for nervous exhaustion. Now I didn't have anyone to look after our three-month-old baby while I did the work I had to do for Masakela, and he was due back in town from a tour. I was terribly upset about what had happened to Shirlee, but I had to regroup in order to work all of this out. Then, during all of my anxieties, I got a telephone call from Masakela saying he was back and that he wanted to meet with me right away. The call made me feel a little better, but not the results of the meeting.

I was excited about the meeting with Masakela, who had just finished an eight-day tour promoting our current release, "Up, Up, and Away," which was showing signs of being a sure hit. This had also been the most successful string of dates we had ever put together, and brought in about eleven thousand dollars. Therefore I was sure Masakela was bringing good news that would make up for what had seemed like a bad day in the beginning. Well, my presumptions were short-circuited when Masakela arrived with Stu Levine, and instead of telling me how successful the trip had been, he began hemming and hawing—the kind you get when something bad is coming.

Then Masakela said it: he wanted to terminate our business relationship because he wasn't satisfied with the way I was directing his career. I was shocked, to say the least, because I knew I had done my best to move Masakela's career. The proof was there in so many ways, including the fact that, in the most recent tally, my investment in Masakela's career had been five thousand dollars, an investment which had negative returns.

Everything that was happening that day was so perplexing. As for Masakela, I didn't try to change his mind, because he seemed so determined. What was important to me was Shirlee in that hospital, my baby Shawn, and what I was going to do about them. So I regretfully said okay to Masakela, but I did remind him of my recent investment and told him I wanted to be paid. He agreed to but never paid me. Because he made the promise but failed to keep it, I held that against him, and I'm not one to hold grudges. I felt I had been taken, and I promised I would never forgive him for doing that, and never let it happen again.

About a year later I met Masakela and we talked about the money, but I don't remember what he said. All I know is there was still no effort to make good what was owed to me. Therefore I continued to censor his role in my show business career, which I even carried into my career in the cookie business. However, as I began to grow spiritually, I realized that it was time to forgive Hugh Masakela. I had reached a point of consciousness in my evolution as a spiritual being which made me realize that forgiveness is the most important function we can perform; forgiving ourselves first, then everybody else for whatever we think they've done. As long as you don't forgive somebody else, you're only holding yourself back. The other person continues living his life. If you forgive, you're free; you're free to accept other things which you were blocking out before the forgiveness. Therefore, by forgiving Masakela, I freed myself.

With Masakela no longer a client, I was without a job, but I did have a safety to fall back on. That was a telephone call I had received several days before from John Levy, who had offered me a job in his personal management firm. Naturally, I had turned it down, since I had no idea what was coming from Masakela. Well, I got on the phone and asked John if the offer was still good, and it was. So the first thing I did was to see about placing Shawn in good hands until everything was worked out. I called Shirlee's mother, Nina, in Raleigh, North Carolina, told her about Shirlee, and asked her if she would look after Shawn. She said she would, and Shawn made his second coast-to-coast flight before he had reached four months. The trip back East allowed me to stop off briefly to visit with Michael and Gregory before flying back to Los Angeles. It was December, and I wanted to spend Christmas Day with Shirlee, who was still in the hospital. Once I had a chance to sit alone and look at what the past several days had brought about, I realized that once again a bad situation did have some good come out of it.

Certainly my joining John Levy's company was something good. First of all, I got to know and work with an absolutely great guy, who paid me a salary of two hundred and fifty dollars per week and loaned me enough money to get settled in a new place before Shirlee came out of the hospital. This turned out to be a one-bedroom apartment in Hollywood, which would be fine for my small family, because Shawn, like my first son, Michael, could sleep in a drawer. I also bought a 1967 Rambler, which would have a story of its own by the time we gave each other up.

For the moment my Rambler shared in the work I was doing for John Levy, which was trying to get his present clients booked on the television variety and talk shows. Also my background in contemporary music, and that whole scene, would help to bring some of those acts to John's firm. The present roster was mostly jazz-oriented, filled with performers who were actually giants in their field: Wes Montgomery, Joe Williams, who had played with the Count Basie Orchestra, Julian "Cannonball" Adderley, and of course Nancy Wilson, who had been the reason I met John Levy in the first place. Nancy was an exceptionally talented singer whom I had tried to represent during my time at William Morris. In pursuing her representation, John and I had had many meetings and became good friends. Now I would be helping her career, and I was very pleased and proud of the opportunity.

My days with John Levy were productive, and I accomplished much of what I had come aboard to do. In my rounds I soon came across a friend of mine from my agency days, Clarence Avant, who had originally been introduced to me by Tom Wilson. Avant had important contacts with the MGM Corporation, among other show business areas, which helped him launch Venture Records. Mickey Stevenson, who as a producer had made important contributions to the success of Motown Records, would run Venture Records, and Avant and Stevenson approached me about managing the acts signed to the label. It was a unique offer, and one that would allow me the opportunity to go out on my own, somewhat, once again. The only problem was my loyalty to John Levy, who had helped me and had taken me in when my career needed time to regroup.

When I informed John of my offer, I once again got an opportunity to find out what was so special about him. He was truly a professional, someone who understood such opportunities. John's encouraging and parting words, "Whatever you gotta do, you gotta do!" would guide many of my career decisions thereafter.

8

*Do not go where the path may lead, but
go instead where there is no path and
leave a trail.*

With John Levy's words reverberating in my mind, I joined
Venture Records in April 1968. The acts I managed were
mostly unknown, with the exception of Kim Weston, who was
married to Mickey Stevenson, the head of Venture. Kim, who
was an excellent singer, had also been with Motown Records
and had recorded with Marvin Gaye. But she had started to
bloom and develop in a big way since leaving Motown, and she
came to the attention of Harry Belafonte, who signed her to
join him on one of his tours. That signing also made it possible for me to meet Belafonte, whom I came to respect for his
responsibility and professionalism as a performer.

Belafonte was a taskmaster, and he worked indefatigably
to maintain his image as a performer. The precision Belafonte
demanded was assurance that his self-contained unit touring
with him would not want for anything that would make their
performance less than *he* wanted it to be. He wanted the best,
because he always wanted to give the public the best. And in
return he expected a lot from the people working for him. It's
one of the reasons he has remained as popular as he is, and
without a series of hit records.

Everything was going fine until Kim's husband, Mickey
Stevenson, decided he could manage Kim better than I.

Therefore, during a date in Cleveland, Ohio, at one of the

theaters-in-the-round, I decided to give up managing Kim Weston. It became clear to me that I would never be able to do any good for her if her husband felt he could do it better. Also, not very much had been accomplished working with the acts on Venture's label, and now that Kim Weston would be handled by her husband I turned my thoughts to trying it alone once again, and seeing if I could be successful as a personal manager.

It was not an easy decision to make, striking out on my own. After all, my first experience as a personal manager had been somewhat disastrous, but a good education. I got a taste of what can happen when you invest wholeheartedly in someone you believe in, only to have him turn around and leave you with nothing but debt. Well, I can take the blame for letting that happen. I had a great deal of naiveté mixed in with my ambition. And I also thought that I had enough experience to be a good personal manager; I did have the potential, but I still had a lot to learn.

That's why, when I ventured into being a personal manager, and my own boss, this time, I thought carefully about what had been missing in me before. One of the elements—that of being a hustler, and striking up a conversation at the drop of a hat—I found in another personal manager named Joey Baker. I had met Joey through Mickey Stevenson shortly before I severed my ties with Venture Records, and it was during that time I realized Joey had something that was missing in me. The reason I was not much of a hustler was probably that I was too shy, insecure, inexperienced, or all of those things. Whatever it was, I could not force myself on people easily, and I knew it. I also knew that if I were going to make it as a personal manager, then I had better learn how, or get somebody else to do it.

Joey Baker was that person. He was perfect at making the pitch, so to speak, while I was good at picking out people and talent to make the pitch to. But even though I now had Joey, I knew I was going to have to change. I had to learn to assert myself more and ask for what I wanted. Otherwise I was wasting my time, and I might just as well go back and work for someone else the rest of my life, and be secure in the fact that I could depend on a paycheck every week. Although I knew what I had to do, I found being a personal manager was not the "piece of cake" I imagined it to be.

Our first and immediate problem was securing clients. Getting a "name act" was not easy because we could not offer them major contacts or the promises of some. Therefore it became apparent that we would have to go after the "unknown acts" because they needed us; they needed a manager because the "established managers" wouldn't have anything to do with them. It really was a natural marriage—us and the "unknown acts"—because they could benefit from my enthusiasm and experience as an agent, which would help to further their careers, and at the same time I could make my mark by helping them develop. But working this way meant our growth was slow, and without hope unless that "unknown act" became a "known act." Also our pockets remained empty because "unknown acts" do not produce income. And as a result we didn't have the money needed to sell our clients. It seemed too true that we needed money in order to make money.

We did have a brief moment of hope for some money when a friend of Joey's brought our firm to the attention of an investment broker named Peter Dunn. He had come across an investment conglomerate looking to get into show business. Therefore Peter combined our personal management company with a motion picture production company as part of a package for these people to invest in. That deal took some time to happen. During that wait my deal with Joey Baker stopped happening.

Joey, as I had known, was a great opener of a business deal, but I later discovered he couldn't, and wouldn't, close a deal. He also had a habit of twisting the truth about certain deals which might have happened, or been saved, if I had been in on the truth about them. So this contributed to many opportunities to make money, and friends, both of which we lost. The more this happened, the more I lost faith in my partner. And by that time I was more assertive and was doing most—

and sometimes all—of the work for our clients. Once I told
Joey I thought we should part company, he agreed. My problem, if I intended to continue alone, was whether I would still
have any clients.

During our brief time together Joey and I had managed to
get two clients we both felt strongly about. They were a folk-
singing group called the People Tree, and an actress-singer
named Pat Finley.

The People Tree were three guys and a girl—Rusty
Harper, Phil Bauman, Bob Fitzgerald, and Brenda Quilling.
They were a self-contained group, in that two of the guys
played guitar and sang; another played upright bass and sang;
and Brenda also did vocals. I was as turned on by them as Joey
was. But most of all I felt they were genuinely nice people
whom I enjoyed working with. It was one of the auditions we
got for the group that brought Pat Finley to our attention.

The audition was at the Horn, a club in Santa Monica
which was sort of a Southern California landmark because of
the well-known talent it had spawned. Such names as Jim
Nabors and Jack Jones got started there. It was the perfect
showcase, because it had a reputation for booking talent, not
names. Managers, booking agents, producers, and just about everyone in the business went to the Horn to see what kind of
talent was appearing on a given night. Therefore the waiting
list for auditions was always long, but we managed to get the
People Tree an audition.

Their audition went well, but they never got the job. We,
however, got a chance to see and hear a cute, pixieish bundle of
personality with a voice and a laugh that demanded attention,
named Pat Finley. We flipped over her, immediately, as did everyone at the audition. Pat was someone I knew I would love to
manage, although I had doubts that would be possible. After
all, she had just come from New York where she appeared in
the Broadway production of *Hello, Dolly!* playing one of the
lead roles. In addition, she had even tried out for the motion
picture version of the musical. Since the Horn was teeming

with my colleagues, I just knew she already had representation. That was one of my first mistakes as a personal manager—taking something for granted.

That's what was good about Joey Baker: he didn't concern himself with what he didn't know. He would always go and ask. So when I told Joey how I felt about Pat Finley, he made the pitch for us to represent her. It was then that we discovered she had an agent but not a personal manager. So, after a few meetings, Pat agreed that we would manage her career. I learned a valuable lesson: you should never take anything for granted. Whatever you believe in you should go after.

Much as I wanted Pat Finley and the People Tree to stay with me after my split with Joey, I was not the kind of person to try and influence their decision. I was really relying on them to understand that I had been doing most of the work for them. They did know, because they elected to keep me as their personal manager. So, with this show of faith in my ability— which still had not been proven—I knew what I had to do. My intuition felt good, and I felt success would be ours now that I had the full reins of my own destiny. What I did not realize was that I would be helped by a minor miracle of sorts.

That minor miracle had almost happened earlier, when Joey and I met Peter Dunn. Well, the first deal had gone sour, but Peter came to me with another deal, which I accepted. This one was firm, so firm I was capitalized with the sum of $110,000, the largest amount of money I had ever received at one time. Thus, Wally Amos and Company, an artist management firm, was formed, and I was now in show business.

I suppose show business had been my goal all the time, although I was more turned on by the *show* than the business, although I did take care of the latter. It was my mistaken belief that *show* was where the profits were; the more you exuded *show* the better the return. So one of the first things I did was get me an expensive wardrobe, which cost $2,500. I wanted to be the epitome of a person doing his *show* thing. I didn't stop with the clothes, though. I also got me an office in Beverly

Hills; actually I got a larger office, since I was already sharing an office in Beverly Hills, and I rented some beautiful furniture. In a way, all that I was doing was being done without thinking clearly. Had I taken a moment to think about all these *show* things I was doing, I would have realized that the only person who was going to benefit from all of this was me— my ego. The people I had to sell my clients to would not be coming to me, not yet anyway.

Nevertheless, I played the role to the hilt. The next business-within-a-business I formed was my own production recording company, which I called Lamplight Productions. This company I put in the hands of Mark Wildey, an Englishman I had met when I was with William Morris. Mark, at the time, was a road manager for the English rock and roll group, the Animals. I saw this recording operation as perfect for my clients, Pat Finley and the People Tree. Completing my cadre of key personnel, I acquired—not hired—an excellent secretary named Sylvia O'Gilvie. She was not easy to get, but I had to have her to complete my move into show business, and I did what was necessary to convince her to join me. In other words, there was no stopping me now. I was getting ready to make a lot of money, although I was spending a lot of money, too.

In addition to the business life, I used this money to boost my personal life. It had always been my feeling that when my position in life improved, which meant getting the kind of money I now had, Shirlee, Shawn, and I would move to a home which was commensurate with that new position. So we found this beautiful two-story house in Hollywood. It was the nicest place I had ever lived in up to that time. I really felt I had arrived.

But, thinking back to that period, I know I was not living a life that was truly *me*. Many of the photographs I took with Shirlee and Shawn bear this out. There I was in my expensive new clothing, posing, but with a look on my face which was unnatural. It was a stern look, with no smile. I guess that was my *show* look. It was what I thought I wanted, this new lifestyle, and it was what I thought Shirlee had always wanted. That was the only reason I did it: I was always trying to do what pleased everyone else, and I was never thinking about what pleased me. Hell, I had no idea *what* would please me. It would not be until I started seeing a psychiatrist that I began giving consideration to what I wanted out of life.

The same feeling prevailed for my clients. There was nothing I wouldn't do to try to get them work. For Pat Finley, one of my first moves was to find her a good agent, with William Morris as the first choice. Due to a lack of experience the People Tree were a different story. Getting work for them was an up and down situation. In the entertainment industry success is measured sometimes by being in the right place at the right time. So timing was what would help their career the most. The People Tree were prepared to wait. They had a barrel of tenacity and were even willing to eat peanut butter and jelly sandwiches—which they were used to eating—until they found work.

Well, appearances on the Joey Bishop and Jonathan Winters television shows gave the People Tree new hope and a chance to change their diet. This was followed by a tour with Joey Bishop, which was great while it lasted but was not very long. The prospects for the future became bleak after this brief "time trial" to try to lengthen their career. So it was back to eating peanut butter and jelly sandwiches, and the People Tree decided to call it quits. They all went home, or wherever, and fulfilled some other dreams. Rusty Harper got himself a wife, a baby, and a Ph.D.; Brenda got a career as an opera singer; Bob, or "Fitz" as we called him, got involved in politics as a campaign manager in his home state of Montana, and Phil went into the business world; he even managed my cookie store in Hollywood for a while.

The loss of one client was followed by the breakthrough of Pat Finley, whose time, it seemed, had come. It was the taste of success I had wanted many times but which had eluded me just as often. And the suddenness of it all, especially since Pat's career as a singer and actress were not happening, only proved that you never know which door will open to let your talent through. Credit for opening that door has to go to Norman Brokaw—Pat's agent at William Morris—for bringing Sheldon

Leonard, a well-known television producer and actor, to see Pat one evening at the Horn. Sheldon was looking to cast an American actress in a series to be produced in England called "From a Birdseye View," which was about two stewardesses. Pat was signed to do the thirteen episodes in London, which meant I would be making my first trip, ever, to London, England. But that trip would not be without purpose; Mark Wildey and I decided we would record an album with Pat while she was in London in order to make a label deal. We just knew the timing was right for that part of her career too.

Prior to Pat's success and my plans to go to London, I had already thought about increasing and diversifying my client list with writers, directors, actors, and singers. A friend of mine, Howard Brandy, who was in public relations, suggested I "take a meeting" (a show business expression) with a writer friend of his named Leroy Robinson, who Howard felt was a nice guy.

When I met Leroy, who at the time was a magazine editor and who was also black, I felt he probably was a qualified writer. He just was not having any luck breaking into television or screen writing. I had never had a writer client before, so I didn't know where to begin, but I figured I would work that out. It was Hollywood in 1969 I was concerned about, since they were still out to lunch as far as minority hiring went. But a Justice Department inquiry, which was going on about the same time, plus some trade paper (*Daily Variety* and the Hollywood *Reporter*) stories indicating there were some producers who wanted to correct these obvious injustices, gave me a direction. I therefore had my secretary get a list of all the producers in Hollywood so I could let them know I had been reading about their search for black writers and that I had one.

While those letters went out in the mail, I took off for London. When I arrived I saw what I had thought I would see, and more. When I was not with Pat on the set of the series, or in the recording studio with her, I was sightseeing, and taking care of my *show* image, which London would be perfect to improve on. To be in London without taking advantage of the fine fabrics and tailors would be criminal, I thought. So I went all the way out and had some suits made by an up-and-coming tailor on Savile Row named Thomas Nutter, who is today one of the top men's designers. I also had shirts with matching ties custom-made at the famous Turnbull and Asser. With these items I felt I had enhanced the myth I had created about my new position in life.

There was another myth, not of my making, which I decided to look into as well. This was the one about English women being partial to black men, and how easy it was to get them and to score. Well, the two weeks I spent in London set me straight on that myth. Because, with all my blackness, my swell-looking suits, and my American importance, the myth remained a myth, since nothing happened. But that didn't shatter me too much, there was still New York, where I had planned to stop before returning to Los Angeles. I felt this was a good time to see Michael, Gregory, and Ruby, plus I would be able to show off my new wardrobe and let everybody see how important I thought I was.

The casualness with which I went about seeing other women while married to Shirlee made me, I know now, the worst kind of person. But I did feel guilty doing it. Nevertheless, I rationalized that Shirlee was not as exciting to me as the women I would fool around with. Because I had this fantasy about show business and my flawless image, plus my need to be a playboy, I felt I should be available to all women. But the women I chased were for romance only. No commitments. I could never make a commitment to any woman, it seemed, not even Shirlee. My cheating also affected the way I communicated with Shirlee. To hide my guilt I would nitpick her, criticize everything she said or did, and although I knew it was because I didn't want to be married anymore I wouldn't admit that.

As for commitments, the only ones I kept were to my sons and to my clients. I never wanted to lose touch with my sons, because I never wanted them to forget that I was their father. When Shawn was born I decided that I would make sure he, Michael, and Gregory developed a good relationship. So maintaining a close relationship with my sons made it easier for me to move further away from Shirlee—something I realize now, but didn't at that time of my life.

At that time I was really engrossed in what I thought was quick success, when I should have realized that none of this was making me money. I was putting out a lot but getting nothing in return. I was, however, optimistic that it wouldn't be too long before I had some returns on my investments. And one of my earlier investments, the letters I sent out about Leroy, my writer, did bring me some returns. A letter from the producer of the television series "Bewitched" resulted in an assignment on that show for Leroy. Then a chance meeting with Sam Denoff, executive producer of another popular television series, "That Girl!" brought yet another writing assignment to Leroy. Sam Denoff was also instrumental in Leroy's selling a story to Bill Cosby, who was then doing a situation-comedy series. The bonus for me was in meeting Sam Denoff and his partner Bill Persky, both of whom became my very good friends; they would come to my rescue many times thereafter.

For the present, however, a certain part of my business was not happening: my record production company, Lamplight Productions. None of the artists Mark Wildey was recording, all of whom were my clients, got any record label deals. Then Mark got together with Danny McCullough, an old friend who had been with the Animals when Mark worked for them and already had a relationship with Capitol Records. I agreed with the opinion that he was a "comer," so I had no qualms about investing money in making Danny happen. I advanced him money constantly, and when he decided he should have a classic automobile (a Bentley) I got my accountant to arrange for him to get a five-thousand-dollar car loan. Well, the biggest hit Danny had was the one that totaled his Bentley. That was also the end of our deal and the beginning of a series of problems which would contribute to my descending to a new low in life.

Meanwhile, I was continuing to meet and sign new clients in an attempt to fill in the losses. John Amos, an actor, comedian, and writer, and Art Metrano, an actor-comedian, were

two of my recent additions. John Amos—who was not related
to me—was brought to me by Leroy Robinson and had been a
former professional football player. I was able to land him his
first network assignment as a comedy writer on "The Leslie
Uggams Show." This was not what he preferred, being a comedian, but it was a beginning. Later I placed him with a commercial agent, and he started doing commercials. When it
came time for John to pay me my commission, though, he refused, since he also had to pay the commercial agent. John did
not understand the roles of agents and personal managers, so I
explained my rights per our contract. If this was not to his lik-
ing, I told him, then I would rather not represent him, and I
was serious. John realized this and asked me to continue, which
I agreed to do, feeling it was just a misunderstanding.

Following that incident I worked very hard to get John
into the area he preferred: acting. His first acting job was on
the "Mary Tyler Moore Show" as Gordy the weatherman, an
infrequent role with dialogue. I heard a new variety series
called "The Funny Side" was being cast. Sam Denoff and Bill
Persky were producing it, so I asked them to cast John in one
of the regular parts. They were reluctant to use John, but I
stayed on them until they agreed to take a meeting with him.

Before any results came out of that meeting with Denoff
and Persky, John decided he wanted to quit show business. I
told him that the chances looked good for "The Funny Side"
and that he should hang in a little longer. But John said he had
made up his mind, and I didn't attempt to change it. Shortly
after that Denoff and Persky contacted me to inform me that
John had gotten the part in "The Funny Side." I told them I
was not representing him any longer, but they could call him
directly. They did, and John went to work, much to my surprise. But I was even more surprised to find out that John had
gotten himself a new manager, and that he was white. John
had been into such a pro-black thing at the time, I couldn't understand why he had dumped me to get himself a white manager. Then, to top it all off, John once again refused to pay me
the commissions I was entitled to for securing his role on "The
Funny Side." I made attempts, both personally and through

Denoff and Persky, but he would not pay me a dime. I then decided this was one Amos I would try to forget.

Years later, after I had started the cookie store in Hollywood, John Amos came into that store. He struck up a conversation with my mother, Ruby, and for some reason gave her twenty dollars, which I asked her to refuse. I told John if he wanted to do something, pay me the commissions he still owed me. Some time later he did pay me. We also had lunch, called a truce, and buried the hatchet. John did go on to establish a pretty decent career for himself as an actor, having played the role of the older Kunta Kinte in "Roots," and being a star on the television series "Good Times."

My big hope, Pat Finley, did not happen as I had hoped. The television series, "From a Birdseye View," did not make the regular season's prime-time schedule and did not fly into everyone's home until the summer as a replacement show. That was unfortunate because the television audience drops in the summer, and without a larger viewership, "Birdseye" flew the coop, so to speak. I watched it, together with maybe a few birds, but we were not enough.

The failure of "Birdseye," though, was not the end of Pat Finley. While her career did not take off as it would have with a hit series, Pat's talent got her important roles in such television series as "The Funny Side" and the very successful "Bob Newhart Show." The major breakthrough never came, however, so Pat eventually shifted her priorities. She lost her desire to be a big star and moved back to Seattle, her hometown. She still performs in local clubs, and there are some guest-starring roles in television movies she's accepted. As for Pat being a major star, I do believe one day she will be. It's just a matter of time before her ship will also come in.

Toward the end of 1969 there were signs of a recession in Hollywood, although Wally Amos and Company had realized this earlier than the rest of the industry. It was apparent to me that my Beverly Hills days were nearly over, however, the optimistic side of me would not allow me to give up just yet—not with one more client up my sleeve.

People, a rock group, I felt was different. For sure, they were different than any other music perfomers on my client list. They had two drummers and also had a name since they had had a hit record on Capitol Records. After some regrouping, they joined Paramount Records, and the company was behind them trying to make it happen for them again. I, too, became committed to that philosophy and helped prepare a do-or-die, all-out blitz of the press and nightclub owners in every part of the country. As always, crusades like this meant more time on the work front and less at home with Shirlee and Shawn.

With People I tried a different approach—I became a showman, which was not my style. With the help of my friend Clarence Avant—a most influential black man, a fantastic human being, and someone everybody knew—I got what I was after. Jim Judelson, president of Gulf & Western, the parent company of Paramount Records, went to see People. I was certain he had never seen the group, or any group with the record company, and wouldn't unless invited. Judelson accepted my invitation, but whether he enjoyed People or not I never found out. It didn't matter once the album came out, because "it wasn't in the grooves," which is what they say when nobody likes the record. It also wasn't in the cards that I should remain with People, and eventually we each went our separate ways. But before that happened two other things changed my life: I separated from Shirlee, and I met a girl named Ula Ness.

Actually, Ula was the reason I separated from Shirlee. She was one of People's most ardent fans, and, like them, a member of the Church of Scientology. Ula Ness was also a Danish model, and one of the most strikingly beautiful women I had ever seen. So I immediately became a fan of hers and, because I knew I would be paying less and less attention to Shirlee and home, I did the inevitable and moved out.

I found a small place, just somewhere I could keep my clothes, because my nights and my leisure time were spent with Ula at her home. When she was away on a modeling job I used her Jaguar XKE, which made me feel important. The XKE was

significant in that it was my last vestige of the *show* image and
Beverly Hills, both of which were slowly becoming things of
the past. It was not too long before Ula became part of my past
as well.

It was because of Ula's involvement with Scientology,
which she tried to involve me in, and her reunion with an ex-
boyfriend, who was also a member, that we finally split. Although, for some time afterward, I did think of her often.

Shortly after my romance with Ula ended, so did the one I
had going with Beverly Hills. It was an awful decision to have
to make after the busy, productive, and educational year 1969
had been for me. But, since it wasn't a profitable year, the
$110,000 capitalization I had received was just about depleted,
and I had no choice. I had no money, or star clients, or potential star clients. I had to give up my *show* image and move to
another station in life, which was a step backward, or so I
thought. It would be several years before I understood that
even then I was moving forward.

9

*Until tomorrow becomes today, men will
be blind to the good fortune hidden in
unfortunate acts.*

Leaving my prestigious station in life, Beverly Hills, to go to
my new and lower station, Hollywood, would have been more
traumatic had I not remembered John Levy's parting and
meaningful words when I left him: "Whatever you gotta do,
you gotta do!"

That was true this time as well, especially since I planned
to continue being a personal manager. The facts were clear: I
had to go where my money would take me. Therefore it would
have to be the small apartment I found in Hollywood, on El
Centro Avenue, which would also serve as my office. It was
cheap, easy to manage, and quaint. I loved the high ceilings of
the huge living room and the single upstairs bedroom, and once
my friends saw my new apartment they were quite envious,
even though I didn't have any furniture. But that didn't bother
me, just as this change was not the end of the world to me. I
did not sit around and feel sorry for myself, nor did I allow
anyone else to. I had been here before—having nothing and trying to get something—and I had survived. Somehow I felt I
would survive this time too.

Getting settled in at El Centro meant spending some
money—which I didn't really have—toward some furnishings. I
did have six hundred dollars budgeted for those things, and a
friend of mine, Ken Fritz, also a personal manager, put me in

touch with a gentleman who found some antique pieces that were perfect. I still needed a carpet and music components, which were in my old Beverly Hills office. So I decided I would go and get them, because, although I had broken my lease, I still had the keys. I went after my carpet and stereo equipment as soon as I could get a van, and the person who installed the equipment went with me. It was done at night—with the van parked in the alley—when no one else was around. I did it this way for the obvious reasons, but I really didn't want anyone to see me make my final exit from a location and role I would frequent and play no more.

Before I knew it, Christmas, 1969, had come and gone, and I was run down. So I decided to take a vacation, with a little of the remaining money, in the one place I knew would help me get my thoughts together, Hawaii. It was twelve years since I had been to these shores, which I had intended to return to after being released from the Air Force. I decided to go to Kauai, perhaps the most beautiful of all the Hawaiian Islands, but there was no sun or warmth or beauty because the weather was awful. It rained every day, and I caught a terrible cold. With nothing to do but look out the window at the rain and the heavy waves in the ocean, I did experience a picturesque moment. It was particularly exciting when two waves would meet and then break up—something like two cymbals coming together. It was beautiful and lyrical, and I felt like writing a poem to describe the moment. My nagging cold, plus my thoughts of what tomorrow would bring, interfered, so I cut my vacation short and returned to the mainland to get down to business.

Helping me to get back to business was my secretary, Sylvia O'Gilvie, who had remained with me. I was lucky to have such a rare person working for me: she was the best secretary anyone could hope for, plus she was a good and devoted friend.

I found that out one day when my Beverly Hills past caught up to me. The Internal Revenue Service found me and let me know there was an outstanding bill of $1,250 owed for some withholding taxes. I didn't have the money when they wanted it, so I asked for an extension, which was granted, and I

thought no more about it. Then a few days later there was a
heavy pounding at my El Centro door. When I answered, two
grim expressions—from a man and a woman—greeted me. They
showed their IRS credentials and, without cracking a smile,
said: "You owe the Internal Revenue $1,250. Are you prepared
to pay?" Of course not. I explained to them I had been granted
an extension, which did not matter. All they wanted was the
payment or they were prepared to put a padlock on the door of
my home/office. That's about the time Sylvia went off:

"Why don't you people leave him alone! He's doing the
best he can . . . he's trying! He works so hard, and he gets so
many bad breaks, but he's still trying!"

I calmed Sylvia when I saw her rage turning to tears. I had
never seen her like this before. But in that short moment I realized what a true friend I had in Sylvia O'Gilvie. She also
showed me how much attention she paid to me and what I was
sincerely trying to do. But I knew that Sylvia's raging request
was like talking to a closed file cabinet, so I told her to gather
certain things of mine, and I would try to find the money for
the IRS. I figured I would jump in my car and go see Sam
Denoff and Bill Persky, who had offices nearby. When I was
leaving, however, I saw a man putting an impound notice on
my car. I asked the man, "Are you going to take my car too?"
He said, "Yes." Therefore I continued on to see if my friends
would also become my saviors. Denoff and Persky did, indeed,
come to my rescue by loaning me the money, and once again
those two fine human beings were endeared to me. But, most
of all, I found that remaining calm and asking myself what was
the solution paid off.

The same condition prevailed when my new station in life
required me to change from a *show* thing to a more natural
way of life for myself. This included putting away the flashy
suits and wearing what I could afford to wear—jeans and T-
shirts, sometimes regular shirts without ties, or suit jackets. It
was also about this time I began to wear Indian gauze shirts
(the kind worn on the Famous Amos package) because they
were easy to wear and keep clean. Wash and wear was also
cheaper. I couldn't afford to have my clothes cleaned, so this

was the way to go. I even stopped wearing socks, primitive as that may sound, since I could also save by not buying socks. Anyway, I knew the no-socks look was okay when Richard Pryor once commented to me: "I see your gloves match your socks."

That transition, or metamorphosis, was as necessary as it was good for me. Removing myself from the unnatural, materialistic life I had led was like removing shackles. However, once that was done I had to get back to business, which meant seeking the kind of talent that would bring me some paydays. Once again, a relationship made in the past paid off.

John Rosica, an old friend who was working at Bell Records, brought a group called Gideon and Power to my attention. They were under contract to Bell and needed a manager. I said I would take a look at them in San Francisco, where they were based. When I saw them perform, I freaked out. Gideon was a kind of preacher—an evangelistic, spontaneous entertainer who wore a bandanna on his head. He was also a black man with two distinct personalities: offstage he was quiet, introverted, and intense, but once he was onstage and the spotlight hit him, so did the spirit. Then he became a person filled with energy and the power to lift thousands out of their seats.

I loved everything about the group. The band, Power, was like a mini-United Nations. They were Filipino, Japanese, Latino, and white; a potpourri of singing and instrumentation. Gideon was the icing on the cake, and this feeling was shared by the Los Angeles *Times* and *Newsweek*. I couldn't believe what Rosica was offering me—Gideon was a dream come true, but, as I would later learn, he could also at times be a nightmare. It was Gideon's chameleonlike personality which made my job as personal manager difficult. But in my desire to make something good out of a bad situation—because there was a solid talent inside that obstinate body—I overlooked Gideon's peculiar ways. That was probably mistake number one.

Another reason we could ignore Gideon's animosities was that his album was soon to be released. We were all excited about its possibilities. Unfortunately, it never made it. We didn't lose faith, though, and looked forward to the next album doing better. But we still had a big problem: no money coming in. I rectified that by contacting a booking agent friend of mine named Rob Heller, who in short order got Gideon and Power a date at San Diego State University. At last, we would make some much-needed money—as long as nothing went wrong with our star, Gideon.

That, however, was wishful thinking on my part. Gideon had found something to become disturbed about, and he closed up during the drive to San Diego. When we got there, Gideon went off by himself. Then, when it was time to rehearse, he couldn't be found. I searched high and low, then I came upon a student who told me he had seen Gideon get into a tax-icab and leave the campus. I was dumbfounded, but sorry for Power, and equally sorry for the kids on campus who were disappointed by the show's cancellation. Also, with no play there was no pay.

Back in Los Angeles, I dropped Power at their motel. I then proceeded to my place at El Centro, where I was going to confront Gideon. His staying at my place was another of my concessions to try to accommodate his moods, and it also saved on an extra motel room. When I arrived at El Centro, Gideon was loading his things into a taxicab and about to get in himself. I called to him, "Hey, man, let's talk." My words fell on deaf ears, because he did not respond. He got into the cab and it drove away, and that was the last time I saw Gideon.

Power became my priority now; they were waiting at the motel for word of what to do, as they were anxious to go home to San Francisco. I couldn't blame them. This latest episode in the Gideon tirades was something they would have to think about. Unbeknownst to them, Gideon had already quit. What I had to decide was how to get them out of their motel without paying, since we had no money to pay the bill. I brought the car into the alley behind the motel and had Power lower their bags from the window. Then they casually walked out of the motel, and at that moment Gideon and Power ceased to exist as my clients.

Unusual personalities and inflated egos were two things I soon realized I would have to face with clients—it went with the territory. But I also came to a point in my career when I decided I would not let a client's ego or personality interfere with my job. An example of what I mean was a client named Abbey Lincoln, who was an actress and a singer. Abbey made her first impression in show business as a singer, doing both popular and jazz songs. Then, later, she became an actress and appeared in a few films before landing a major co-starring role with Sidney Poitier in *For Love of Ivy*. In both media Abbey commanded attention because as a singer she was always original, and as an actress she exuded a peculiar kind of charm. Eventually, though, attention seemed to slip away from Abbey, and her career took a vacation, so to speak. When I met her, and she agreed to let me represent her, it was my intention to make something happen again with both of her careers.

First of all, I put her with my old standby, William Morris, because they were also interested in Abbey and felt they could get her work. In the back of my mind was the thought that acting jobs would naturally open the door for a recording contract. When I received the call telling me Abbey had been offered a role on one of the most popular series on television, "Bewitched," and for $1,500 a week—the top salary for guests appearing on the show—I knew things were moving in a right direction. Well, Abbey proved me wrong—after I called her with the offer, she said, "That's not enough money. I'm a star." I was floored. I couldn't believe what I was hearing, and she wouldn't change her mind even when I explained what this all meant.

Therefore I made the decision not to impose my opinions on Abbey any longer, and on that same telephone call I said to her: "We're going to have to terminate our relationship. Let's call it quits, Abbey," and I said nothing after that. I just hung up the telephone. My next move was one of maturity for me, because I took all of her photographs and biographies to her apartment and left them at the desk, along with my good wishes for her future success.

All the moments of my personal management days were not studies in personalities, egos, and stubbornness. There were moments when I was totally pleased, satisfied, and gratified. But, because of the rarity of those moments, a young, talented comedian named Franklyn Ajaye brings a smile to my face whenever I remember working with him.

I first saw Franklyn at the Comedy Store, a popular club for new comedians, at the suggestion of Burt Metcalfe, who was at that time casting director of the television series "M*A*S*H" and who went on to become the executive producer.

When I saw Franklyn, I had to agree with Burt that he was funny, even though he was a beginner and his talent was undeveloped. I felt Franklyn could use me, but getting him to agree took some convincing words from me. His worry was that he had heard bad things about managers, mostly that they rip clients off, which is sometimes true. I laid my cards on the table, telling him of my interest in my clients and just how far I was willing to go with my commitment. It was enough, whatever I said, and Franklyn Ajaye became my client.

I didn't waste any time confirming all I had said to Franklyn, which meant exhausting every contact I had. This included a position I had as talent coordinator on a television series called "Black Omnibus," which starred James Earl Jones. Franklyn appeared on the series, making his national television debut as well. Then I got a booking for Franklyn at the Troubadour in Hollywood as the opening act for singer Jerry Butler, which was also Franklyn's first club appearance, other than the Comedy Store. This resulted in a turn of events which would benefit Franklyn's career as well as enhance my own.

In the audience was Jerry Moss, the chairman and the "M" of A&M Records (the "A" represents Herb Alpert). He liked Franklyn's comedy routines and decided to have Franklyn record for his label. I was overjoyed. But I was overwhelmed when Jerry asked me to produce the album. Modesty made me question my ability to produce an album. Later, after thinking about it, I decided, "Hell, what d'you have to know to produce? If you like the material that you're producing, you can advise the artist where the good parts are, or where it can be improved." Well, by then I knew Franklyn's material, so I took on the challenge of being a record producer.

Being the producer for my client placed me in the best position I had ever been in during my show business career. When we decided to record a live album at the Comedy Store, it was, unbeknownst to me, a good decision. The A&M promotion men from around the country would be in Los Angeles at the same time holding their summer conference. I invited them to the recording session so they could hear, first hand, what Franklyn and his material were all about, and they would generate enthusiasm for the product before it was ready. However, there was a danger to all of this. If Franklyn was not good that night, then the deal and plans could go sour. I was confident it would come off well, but Franklyn was scared to death.

I didn't blame him for feeling the way he did. After all, not long before this young, intelligent, first-time comedian who had dropped out of Columbia University's Law School had been trying to make a living as a salesman. Well, Franklyn was funny enough to sell them, and in making an album that they, in turn could sell, I got my first taste of the editing room, which was a great education, thanks to my engineer, Steve Mitchell.

Promoting the album was next, and it wasn't easy. It was a great experience for me *and* Franklyn, who improved his act during the promotional tour. I never missed a performance, and I feel I learned a lot about comedy just by being there. I would also critique each of Franklyn's performances, letting him know what worked and what did not. Being his eyes and ears taught me an invaluable lesson, one that is still paying off for me doing my own promotions on behalf of Famous Amos Chocolate Chip Cookies. For sure, the comedian in me was enhanced by paying such close attention to Franklyn Ajaye.

One other thing I found to be true: success brings attention. Thus, other comedians saw me working with Franklyn and asked me to manage them. I refused, because Franklyn was the only comedian I wanted. Gil Friesen, however, a vice-president at A&M, asked me to manage a singer named Mississippi Charles Bevel, and I accepted since A&M had been so good to me. I found that I liked both Bevel's music and Bevel himself, because he seemed so responsible and straightforward.

With all that going for Bevel, it was easy for me to make a commitment to his career.

One thing I did not learn when I talked with him was his dislike for tours. But he was at his best when on the road, performing. I also liked the fact that he had not been spoiled by the negative aspects of show business—which was a plus for Franklyn Ajaye—and I could see another winner on my hands. Therefore I felt good. In fact this was one of the few times in a long time I had. So I decided to take a much-needed vacation with my three sons to the Grand Canyon, which would include a side trip to Denver to see Franklyn, who was performing there. The trip was one of the greatest I ever took with my sons. However, my return to Los Angeles and some unexpected news did dampen my high spirits.

It turned out Bevel did not want to record anymore or make personal appearances. In essence, Mississippi Charles Bevel wanted out of show business. My first reaction on hearing this was that I had another John Amos situation. I just knew Bevel's success, which I had contributed to, had attracted another manager, and I was losing him for that reason. So I talked with Gil Friesen, and he confirmed Bevel's intentions: he definitely wanted out of the business. Bevel's decision, therefore, got my utmost respect because of the courage he showed in making it.

When it's good, it's great, but when it's bad, it seems to get worse. That's how I felt after learning that A&M was not picking up Franklyn Ajaye's option to record more albums. Franklyn's second album had not done as well as the first, and I understood the rules: if you don't sell records, they don't continue to record you. So, without a client on the label, I was asked to vacate my office on A&M's lot. This turn of events started me to thinking about what it all meant, and just where was I going?

It was October 1974, thirteen years since I had started at the William Morris Agency. I had been on my own as a personal manager for six years, and, basically, I was doing the same thing. I would put all my hopes in my clients, and then nothing would happen. It was like being on a treadmill; you're walking but you're going nowhere. Then you run, and you're still not getting anywhere. When I projected into the future, I saw myself ten years down the road doing the same thing, calling up producers and casting agents to tell them about these great acts I had—which I never doubted—and having the same results. I was tired of never having any money and never knowing how I was going to get money to pay my expenses.

My personal, married life was also something I considered. It, too, was like the treadmill syndrome. Marriage had been a here-today, gone-tomorrow situation too many times. Nothing was being resolved, and the relationship had just about dissolved between me and Shirlee after I returned home a second time. Therefore I decided to leave for good because I felt it would be the best for Shirlee, Shawn, and me.

Things remained up in the air for me; I had not yet committed myself to a change, but something was obviously in the wind, even though I took on other clients. But after a while my not making any money with my clients, plus some of my clients not paying me my commissions, finally got to me and, thinking more about that treadmill I seemed to be on, I made the decision to call what I was doing to a halt.

That was it, I told myself. I had to do something else; something that I could benefit from. It was not happening in show business for me, so I would be better off out of it. Where I would go or what I would do was not yet formulated in my mind. Whatever it was, I felt I was ready for it. I had been prepared to do just about anything. But, for now, I was going to discontinue being a personal manager.

10

"A *thousand-mile journey begins with the first step.*"

—CONFUCIUS

My decision to get off the show business treadmill did not come about because a few of my clients were slow paying my commissions. They were the catalysts, for sure, but the idea had been in the works for a month before my final decision.

It occurred during my early September 1974 vacation with my sons, Michael, Gregory, and Shawn. The four of us had jumped into my old and faithful 1967 Rambler ("Amos La Plume") to get out of Los Angeles and leave show business behind; at least for a week, anyway. Sitting on the south rim of the Grand Canyon, with all its beauty, its breathtaking serenity, vast countryside, and space, my thoughts were transported back in time.

I thought about the kind of life I had been living for almost thirteen years, which was my show business life. I related it to the song, "That's Life,"—one month I was riding high, and the next I was shot down. I thought to myself, "My God, I've been doing show business for *so* long! What I'm doing is going nowhere. I'm up one moment, down the next." Funny I should think like this, because I had not expected, or anticipated, anything going wrong in the near future; I was on a roll, so to speak. In retrospect I can see that I was definitely being directed in a different direction, although I didn't know it at the time.

I still was not cognizant of that force pulling me when I returned to Los Angeles from the Grand Canyon, but eventually I realized a change was imminent and I had to do *something!*

One day while sharing my "What am I gonna do now?" blues with a secretary at A&M named Pam Blackwell, she told me she, too, was ready to do something else. But Pam didn't know what that was. So we jokingly decided that maybe we could do something together: "Maybe we should go to Carmel and live in peace," and "Yeah, and let's open up a cookie store!" were some of our wild thoughts. It was just conversation. I had no romantic interest in Pam or she in me. We were just good friends, maybe because I would bring some of my homemade chocolate chip cookies to her—as I did for most of the personnel at A&M—and she would occasionally loan me money.

Continuing my idea of doing something else, I even thought about going to work for someone else doing public relations or developing talent at a record company. The thought of returning to the William Morris Agency even crossed my mind. It took a little while before anything came together, although I never stopped searching for a path that would allow me to get in step with the rhythm of life and its flow. Then I found it.

It happened one evening while I was enjoying some of my homemade chocolate chip cookies with B. J. Gilmore, who was Quincy Jones's secretary at A&M Records. While we munched on my cookies I was having my usual thoughts about what to do, and what I could do that wasn't in show business. Suddenly B.J. said, in her slow, calm southern drawl, "Why don't we go into business together selling your chocolate chip cookies?"

I looked at B.J., both smiling and thinking, and responded with, "That's a great idea. But I don't have the money." B.J. said she did; that is to say, B.J. felt she could get the money from a friend of hers who was the owner of a well-known fast food franchise in Los Angeles called Tommy's Hamburgers. The idea of selling my cookies excited me. It had been put to me many times when I took them around as part of my "good

will" gestures to casting agents, producers, and the like, but I
never imagined that I would take the suggestion seriously. But
now that B.J. had made me feel that it would not be an impos-
sibility—opening a store and selling my homemade chocolate
chip cookies—I became committed to the idea.

When I was a youth I was happily committed to eating
my Aunt Della's chocolate chip cookies. In fact hers were the
only chocolate chip cookies I would eat. Somehow I must have
thought I would never be without them, because I never got
the recipe, and when I moved to Los Angeles I was at a loss
since Aunt Della's cookies were no longer available. So I simply
went without. I was not going to buy the chocolate chip cookies in stores, because I didn't feel they were authentic. Besides,
once you've eaten a homemade chocolate chip cookie you don't
want to eat anything else. That was my problem, not having
Aunt Della's cookies nor being able to make my own. However,
to satisfy my cookie cravings, I did try Orbits, another kind of
cookie, and the only kind I dared to eat.

Then good fortune came my way in 1970, thanks to a client named Shari Summers who came to my office munching on
chocolate chip cookies she had made. I asked her to let me
taste one, and it tasted great! I didn't know what to make of
this cookie, since I had never tasted *anyone's* homemade cookies other than Aunt Della's. I was so excited, I demanded that
Shari give me the recipe. She told me it was on the back of the
Nestlé's chocolate morsel bag. I didn't believe her. But what I
really couldn't believe was how long I had deprived myself by
not knowing about that recipe. I could bake. Had I known
about the recipe, how complete my life would have been. Well,
I made up my mind. So that evening I went to the market and
picked up everything I needed, including that Nestlé's package,
and excitedly baked my first batch, ever, of chocolate chip cookies. Talk about Christmas coming early!

After I mastered the baking of them, they became my
show business "hook." I would take them with me whenever I
had a meeting with someone to sell a client, and they would

work like magic. More doors than I ever imagined were opened all because of my homemade chocolate chip cookies. Before long I had an industry-wide reputation because of my homemade cookies. However, as famous as I was because of my chocolate chip cookies, they could never induce enough people to employ my clients.

Since I had already told B.J. to get busy locating her friend with the money, the next morning I was anxious to get started. That's the way it is with me. Once I make a commitment I don't like to procrastinate. There's a certain energy existing when you get an idea, and unless you act on it you will lose it. I didn't want to lose this idea, so I demanded that we get started. But where do you start? Well, I didn't have to start at the beginning, I found out. Having the idea to go into business could be called the beginning, just like having the money. Well, I had one out of those two, but there were many other things I needed to do in order to get started. First, I had to find out what the health requirements were for opening a cookie shop. This I asked B.J. to check out, along with some other details. While she did that I baked cookies, which was something I always did anyway. I baked them primarily because I liked to eat them. Also, I didn't mind giving them away, because that was my way of sharing, and the surest way for everyone to remember me. So the idea of selling cookies was just a natural extension of the earlier me. Now when I visited A&M Records and passed out cookies, it was also to spread the word about my new venture.

Roland Young, who was the creative director at A&M, whose main responsibility was designing concepts for album covers, was one of the people I gave some cookies to. I also told him of my plans to open a cookie store. "Well, if you do, let me do the graphics," Roland quickly offered. I had never thought of needing graphics, although I had envisioned putting a photograph of my son Shawn, or all three of my sons, on the bag or whatever would hold the cookies. But serious graphics never entered my mind. Once again, where was the beginning?

Word of what I was planning to do was spreading just as I was spreading my homemade cookies around. My dream, how-

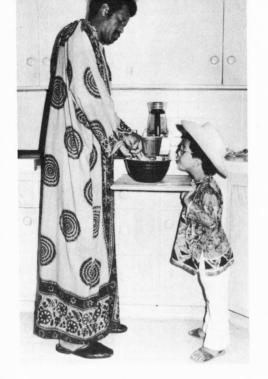

Top left: Baking cookies at home. Shawn waits impatiently for the finished product.

Bottom: The original invitation to the "premiere" of the superstar cookie . . .

Announcing

the premiere of

The Delicious — The Delectable

THE **Famous Amos**
CHOCOLATE CHIP COOKIE

Sunday, March 9, 1975 — 1 P.M. to 5 P.M.

7181 Sunset Blvd.
(2 blocks west of La Brea)

Bring your family and/or friends

Attendants will park those cars that
arrive with drivers. (No exceptions.)

—Wally "Famous" Amos

P.S. Of course, chocolate chip cookies will be served.

Top right: "Amos and Andy" at the Los Angeles Famous Amos store, where Andy Warhol autographed and sold his book to benefit Literacy Volunteers of America. (Photo by Jim Frank)

Bottom: Roderick Sykes, Jeff Bridges, Wally Amos, Herb Alpert, Rozzell Sykes, and Mayor Tom Bradley link arms and energy at St. Elmo Village.

Top left: Wally and Christine at her art show in Hawaii.

Bottom: Wally with Ruth Colvin, founder of Literacy Volunteers of America, and Dennis Gooler, former president. (Photo by Kwame Brathwaite)

Top right: Holding the ladder for the mayor of Nutley as the street is renamed Chocolate Chip Way. Who wouldn't want to live *there?*

Bottom: Waving to the crowd from a giant snail in the Macy's Thanksgiving Day Parade, 1980. (Photo by Ron Lynch)

ever, was almost shattered by the indication from B.J. that she
might not be able to come through with her investor friend
after all. Therefore I began to think of some money sources of
my own. I didn't intend to quit now. I loved the idea too
much, including the possibility of eating chocolate chip cookies
whenever I pleased, while making a living at the same time.

Meanwhile I still had a few clients to service, although my
client list had diminished greatly. I still had to do whatever I
could to find work for them and to make some money. This
was not easy, since I didn't want to put off the Cookie Trip, as
I referred to it. My philosophy about relationships being important turned out to be my savior. It was almost like a pattern,
which was not recognizable to me at the time, that whenever I
found myself in a bad situation, or in need of help, my good
past relationships would always be there. These people always
remembered me as being a consistent hard worker, and honest
with whomever I did business. Those were my primary charac-
teristics, and because there were people who recognized that in
me, they would help me get from one stage of my life to the
next.

Such was the case with Sam Trust. He ran ATV Music, a
publishing house which licensed all of the Beatles music. I had
met Sam when he was manager of Beechwood Music, the publishing arm of Capitol Records, and since that time he had always come into my life just when I needed him. Just after leaving A&M's lot, he came into my life and gave me an office and
a job. Sam hired me to develop new artists for his Granite Records and publishing company. He also allowed me to pursue
work for my remaining clients and relieved most of the pressure
of making a living while developing my cookie business. This
allowed me to think seriously about the proposal and what ingredients it should have. For sure, I wanted it to whet appetites
enough so that investors would participate lavishly. I already
knew two potential investors who were hooked on my cookies,
my longtime friends Helen Reddy and her husband, Jeff Wald.

Over the years Jeff, Helen, and I had become increasingly
better friends. I first met Jeff when I was an agent at William
Morris, and we were reunited when he moved to Los Angeles

and went into personal management with Helen Reddy, his wife, as his client. By then, our friendship had grown stronger, and Jeff and Helen would, on occasion, babysit Shawn whenever Shirlee and I had to go somewhere. Whenever I was taking a business trip to New York I would take their daughter, Tracy, back with me to visit her grandparents, Jeff's mom and dad. Most of all, Jeff and Helen loved my homemade chocolate chip cookies. Also, if I was baking I'd call them, and Jeff would drop down to my house and get some cookies as fast as they would come out of the oven. Jeff, however, would get cookies for Helen, and raw dough for himself, which he loved to eat, and which I still give him today.

Since I knew Jeff and Helen were in the dough, thanks to Helen's initial hit record, "I Am Woman," plus they were good friends who loved my cookies, I began to put my proposal together with them firmly in mind as the first investors I would approach. But I had no intentions of taking advantage of that friendship by not being organized. After all, I was asking them to put their money into something that I believed in. Loaning me money was nothing new for Jeff and Helen. By the time I approached them to invest in my cookie business, my initial indebtedness to them amounted to $1,500. Obviously, the old adage about the best way to lose a friend being to loan him money did not apply to Jeff Wald and Helen Reddy.

From October to December of 1974 I thought about making the transition from mixing my cookie batter in a small bowl to mixing it in a larger one, and going from homemade to commercial cookies without losing the homemade taste. In other words, I realized that my chocolate chip cookies would have to be commercialized, so the proper equipment would have to be purchased. That meant I would need a large mixer, an oven, a larger refrigerator, a large worktable, and a scale to measure out my ingredients.

Meanwhile I was faced with choosing a name for my cookie business. Once again B. J. Gilmore, who had planted the idea of the business in my head, suggested "Famous Amos" as the business name. This was natural since B.J. was one of a few people to call me "Famous Amos." Oscar Brown, Jr., who had been a client, was the person to dub me Famous Amos. The birthplace of that name was in Washington, D.C., during one of Oscar's performances there. After Oscar's performance many visitors showed up backstage to wish him well, many of whom knew me and spoke to me. After a while my popularity was noticed by Oscar, who responded to it with, "Damn, Famous Amos."

Anyway, B.J.'s suggestion of a name was rushed by me to Chuck Casell, a good friend who worked in the creative department at A&M as a writer. I said, "Man, we got a name. It's Famous Amos Chocolate Chip Cookies store, shop, or whatever." Chuck didn't say a thing. He just wrote, "*The* Famous Amos Chocolate Chip Cookie." The old lightbulb went on and I knew we had a name.

Next came my philosophy about The Cookie, which was aimed at people who would work for it. I saw these people as "Friends of The Cookie," and my philosophy was that anyone who became a part of that illustrious group would have to taste The Cookie first. I wanted everyone involved with The Cookie to experience its quality and charm by tasting it.

One time when my "Friend of The Cookie" philosophy paid off was when I bought my ingredients from a veteran salesman named Leo. He was the I-know-it-all-type salesman and had been at his line of work for a long time; much longer than I, naturally. Therefore, when I asked him to taste The Cookie, Leo didn't think he needed to. "I know just what you need, kid," was all he said. Well, Leo clarified my reason for using the taste philosophy, because if I intended to make a quality cookie the way I thought it should be made I had to make sure I was getting the ingredients I needed. What I didn't need was ingredients "that all bakeries use," which was Leo's suggestion.

There was one other thing I realized right away. I was not really leaving show business, nor would I be giving up *all* my personal management clients. Not with The Cookie, which I had already called, to tease the public, the "superstar of cookies." So to establish that fact it had to be promoted very well. I realized I would also have to manage The Cookie, just as I would any other client. Why not? After almost fourteen years as an agent and personal manager, if I couldn't do what was necessary to make my cookies the superstars I knew they were, then no one could.

Shortly after I had gotten all the prices for equipment and ingredients, and projected my promotional plans, I plugged all of this into my proposal. Nickel-and-diming here and there, I arrived at a start-up budget of $25,000. I figured $20,000 to get the store open, and the other $5,000 would help to keep me alive and my creditors at bay until the store was in operation. There was a great deal of naiveté in this budget, which I had no way of knowing at the time. I had made a commitment and I had to follow through.

It was in December 1974 that all my notes for the proposal were ready, so I could commit them to a formal proposal. The fourteen pages of creative writing flowed easily, and I was entertained while typing it. I hoped that whoever read it would also be just as entertained, and tempted enough to take a bite.

Actually, that was a literal possibility, because at the opening of the proposal was a package of various cookies—chocolate chip with pecans, chocolate chip with peanut butter, and butterscotch chip with pecans—which I planned to sell. In addition to giving the potential investor an opportunity to get a taste of what they would be putting their money into, I felt they should understand my sense of humor and maybe get a good laugh as well. After all, how many serious proposals are also capable of making the investor laugh? I also placed cookies at the end of the proposal so readers finished up laughing and wanting more of my chocolate chip cookies.

When my proposal was ready, my "sure thing" investors, Helen Reddy and Jeff Wald, were not. They were out of town. Meanwhile I went after two other investors I had on my list. They were Sam Trust, my savior at ATV Music, and Cliffie Stone, a legend in the country music field, and also at ATV. Both Sam and Cliffie had expressed interest while I was putting the proposal together. However, when I delivered it to them, they both had second thoughts; Sam didn't have the capital to put out, and Cliffie just wasn't sure. Therefore I decided to wait for Helen and Jeff, and to continue to pull various other pieces of my dream together.

Meetings were held between Roland Young, a salesman at Crown Zellerbach, the paper company, named Steve "Shaky" Weinberg, and myself about the packaging of the cookies. Also an independent photographer named Harry Mittman was taking photographs of The Cookie—the same photographs, incidentally, that are now seen all over the world. There was also a photograph to be taken of me, by a well-known commercial photographer named David Alexander—the "natural Wally Amos," Roland called it; he used it for his design of me presenting The Cookie.

The money needs were crucial, especially when I found a store I liked but didn't have the deposit. It was on a busy street —Santa Monica Boulevard—in West Hollywood, and had just been renovated. The size of the store seemed right, although I was guessing, since I had never put a cookie shop together before. I was also guessing when I went to Tom Patchett and Jay Tarses, the producers of "The Bob Newhart Show," whom I had met when they were stand-up comedians, to borrow money for the deposit on the store. Well, my guess was right, because they did, in fact, loan me the money. Once again a former good relationship paid off.

I was still in need of a few more dollars in order to provide some kind of Christmas for my family. But I had absolutely no money. Then one day a good friend of mine named Rozzell Sykes showed up at my El Centro office. He was just in time to hear my laments about no money for Christmas. Rozzell, who was always broke himself, said he had $100 which he wanted to give me half of. It was a generous gift, and typical of the person giving it. And Rozzell was not the only person who felt the spirit of the season. With all the good fortune I had at the end of the year I felt confident that the next year, 1975, would be my year for sure.

About a week into the new year my prophecy came true. Jeff Wald and Helen Reddy returned to Los Angeles, and their secretary, Paula, told me to bring my proposal to her and she would see that they got it right away. Later that day I checked my answering service, and there was a message from Jeff Wald stating that he ". . . wanted chocolate chip cookie rights for the world."

When I met with Jeff at his home, I started to give him a full sales pitch—something I had been preparing myself to do for the last three months—but he cut me off, telling me that I didn't need to sell him or Helen. They knew me, and that was enough. Well, with that attitude I decided to ask him for the entire budget, $25,000. Jeff said all he could go for was $10,000, because his business manager, whom he listened to, was not as positive about his investing in chocolate chip cookies as he was. The truth was, Jeff and Helen were investing in me because I was their friend. Their desire to see me succeed was the reason for investing in me at this time.

Not only did Jeff and Helen come up with a good portion of the budget, they helped by getting a friend of theirs and mine, Artie Mogull, a recording executive, to put up $5,000. This was perfect, because prior to Mogull's offer I had been in contact with Jerry Moss, the head of A&M Records, and he had also wanted in for $5,000, plus he was also going to get his partner, Herb Alpert, to go in for $5,000. With those commitments, I was on my way. Picking up the initial $15,000 from Jeff's and Artie's business manager, however, was not easy.

Jeff had warned me that their business manager was not keen on investing in chocolate chip cookies, so when I went to pick up the check I was left waiting for four or five hours. I remained patient, but it didn't matter because I never got the check. So I went away and returned the next day, and again I sat patiently until Ed Gross, the business manager, finally gave me the check. I understood the role Ed had to play as a business manager, and how cautious he had to be on behalf of his clients, but I felt Ed was overstepping his responsibility by not doing what Jeff and Artie had decided they wanted to do.

Anyway, with the first $15,000 in tow I was now able to get started in developing for real what was on paper and in my mind. One thing that had slipped my mind was what kind of furniture would go in the store. Just as I hadn't realized I would need graphics, I wasn't thinking of how much the furniture in the store would contribute to the ambience. Well, it's a good thing I had a neighbor named Tony Christian, who happened to be an artist and a lover of my cookies. On a certain afternoon I invited Tony over to my apartment to sample some chocolate chip cookies with peanut butter, and I told him about my plans for the store. During our conversation Tony started telling me how he saw the shop, with lots of plants, wood, and warmth, just like the living room of my home—someplace I could sit down and talk to people for the first time with the feeling I had known them all my life, while eating chocolate chip cookies. Tony's ideas were a mirror image of my thoughts, and I knew he was the one to design the interior of the cookie shop. Tony agreed, but he had one request: that I not try to see what he was doing until he was finished. I reluctantly agreed.

But just *where* Tony's designs would go became a problem I had not anticipated. I lost the Santa Monica store, even though I had put a deposit down and had a lease. Well, like they say, you can't fight City Hall, because that's exactly who wanted my store. But losing the Santa Monica store opened the door for me to go into a better store in a better location: Sunset Boulevard, the Strip.

It's interesting how things work out. The best part of this new place, other than being on the Strip, was the building: it had once been a House of Pies, among other types of eateries, so the layout was suitable for my own plans. What I had to do was convince the present lessee, Barish Chrysler, a car dealership, to sublet it to me. My enthusiasm, plus my dropping names like Helen Reddy, Jerry Moss, and Herb Alpert, and my cookies, naturally, were able to convince Bud Barish to give me a lease, effective February 1, 1975. Tony Christian was excited by the space available in this Sunset Boulevard store, but I still was not allowed to see what he was building in his garage.

Chuck Casell, a very creative human being and one of my inspirations, as well as a dear friend, was someone I just knew would be as happy as I was to find this new location.

"It's a bad-luck corner," was Chuck's initial reaction. "It's not gonna happen if you have it on that corner," he decided, because so many other businesses had failed there. So, rather than argue with Chuck, I took him to the corner he was calling a white elephant.

"Now tell me, Chuck," I asked as we stood on the corner of Sunset Boulevard and Formosa Avenue, "how can a corner, this corner, be bad luck? The corner didn't do anything to anyone. This corner was meant to house a cottage, a cookie cottage. I can just see it."

But Chuck was still unconvinced, and this troubled me, so I tried pointing out some other things: "Look, Chuck, it's dirty now, but once we clean it up, you'll be able to see how the furniture and the walls Tony's building will look. It will be a friendly place . . . a friendly corner . . . that everyone will want to come to, to visit with The Cookie." Chuck's opinion was important to me, and I respected it and him. After all, he had shared this vision with me, often, and I wanted him to see the potentials of this corner and store just as I had. After some more word portraits from me, Chuck started to see, and I felt better, even if he wasn't completely sold. I was convinced that once the store was cleaned he'd see it too.

But cleaning the store—the broken glass and cigarette butts both inside and outside the premises—was not an easy job. That first day I only had Shawn, my eight-year-old son, to help. The next days my mother Ruby, who had moved to Los Angeles, and my associate Ellen Cullum came in, and we got it together. Then I put a sign in the window saying: THE COOKIES ARE COMING! THE COOKIES ARE COMING! MARCH 9TH.

Around February 15, a month before the opening, I needed the balance of the budget, $10,000, from Jerry Moss and Herb Alpert. We had not completely used up the initial $15,000, but it was going faster each day. I called Jerry to see when I could expect the check and got the unexpected. He told me that he would be unable to put up the money after all because he had overextended himself in some other financial deals. Needless to say, the bottom fell out of my plans. But despite my disappointment, I chose not to do the obvious, which would have been to try to change Jerry Moss's mind. Instead I went to work to find a replacement.

Starting at the As in my address book, and leafing through until I came across a potential investor, brought me to singer Marvin Gaye. I had known Marvin when I was an agent and he was with Motown Records during the early days of his career. We became friends during that time, and through the years we occasionally ran into each other. Finding Marvin wasn't easy, although Motown wasn't a bad place to start. It turned out he had his own office, so I called him. He wasn't there, so I left a message that he call me because it was important.

Next I found Ned Tanen's name, who was president of motion picture productions at Universal Studios. Ned and I had first met when I managed Hugh Masakela—and Ned had been in charge of UNI Records, which Masakela recorded for. Ours had also been a loose friendship, but finding him was not difficult. I told him what I was looking for and got a positive response—he even invited me over to his office. When I arrived Ned was still in a meeting, so I called the Hollywood store to see if I had heard from Marvin Gaye, which I had. I called Marvin immediately and wasted no time making my spiel. Marvin cut me off, saying I didn't need to sell him; he liked the idea, and he would put $5,000 into it. Happy with this news, I promised him I would get the proposal and other information over to him before the day was out. "That's cool," Marvin said. "You don't have to do that. I know you, Wally, and it's okay. I'm in for $5,000."

With Marvin's money set, I went in to see Ned Tanen feeling cocky. I just knew that Ned would be my last stop. Ned did want to help me, but he said he didn't have the money. However, he felt Roger Smith—Ann-Margret's husband/personal manager—did, and he would contact him for me. The next day I called Ned, and the news was not what I wanted to hear: he didn't have any luck with Roger Smith. So I had to press on, quickly, because we were only ten days from the opening. That prompted me to play a hunch: I decided to see if Marvin might have an extra $5,000, which I would pick up the same time I got the original $5,000 he had already committed.

I was right. Marvin did have the money. He also had a

different hat on this time—he was now the businessman, and he wanted to know if he was going to get a larger percentage for his $10,000. Marvin also knew that time was running out for me and that he was in a good position to negotiate. I couldn't blame him—friendship aside, this was business. So I gave him the extra points because I needed his money. I figured a smaller percentage of something was better than a larger percentage of nothing.

Prior to completing my list of investors, I had gotten my attorney, Ray Tisdale, to incorporate the cookie business. Ray had not been too high on my plans to start a cookie business because his background had been with large corporations, and tried and true investments. There was no background for a major success in the kind of business I was getting into, according to Ray. He did, eventually, come around to accepting what I was doing, and his description of the corporation in the articles of incorporation proved he'd become a "Friend of The Cookie":

(1) The specific business in which the corporation is primarily to engage is to develop, bake, market, distribute through retail and wholesale channels, and otherwise exploit cookies especially chocolate chip cookies, developed and baked with blissful care in strict compliance with *recipes created through love and patience by Wally Amos with the assistance of his discriminating taste buds.*

It was obvious to me that he too had been infected by the brown fever I had been spreading.

The next order of business for this business was to get the word out that we would be sharing the arrival of The Famous Amos Chocolate Chip Cookie. That would require a media blitz of sorts to let everyone know that a superstar had arrived on the scene. Therefore I sent out 2,500 invitations—or challenges, possibly—to the store's opening, most of which were hand-delivered by me. Included with my invitation was a biography of me specially written by Bud Scopo (an A&M employee), which I still use today, a photograph of me and a photo of The Cookie (8 × 10 glossy befitting a star in show business). Also befitting this superstardom, I got permission from A&M and the William Morris Agency to use their logos on the photograph of The Cookie. This was to indicate that The Cookie had a recording contract and agency representation. The Cookie also had its own biography, which was specially written by Jay Michels, a vice-president in NBC-TV promotions, West Coast, and some of his staff. In other words these people *wanted* to spread brown fever, because they were *that* infected by The Famous Amos Chocolate Chip Cookie.

As the time drew nearer to opening day, only important bits and pieces concerning the cookie shop were left to do. Primarily, there was Tony Christian's creation, which I was dying to see. When I finally did, I saw everything we had envisioned: the counter, the chairs, the special wood walls, the solid oak parquet floor, the tables, the color, the lighting, and the ambience. I was almost speechless, except for my happy comment, "What a labor of love!" It was all of that and more, including a specially made case for the mixing bowl and spoon I had used at my home: symbols of my beginnings as a chocolate chip cookie maker. My eyes could not believe the richness I was beholding. Also my heart refused to believe that this supercreative friend of mine, Tony Christian, had made my store's interior for only $4,000. Tony's girlfriend Norma would not be left out of this special event, so she created the beautiful plants outside and inside the store. This required hours of digging and planting, incorporating her own love with the love that never seemed to stop from all the "Friends of The Cookie."

One week before we opened I was afforded yet another wonderful experience. Actually, my heart almost stopped this particular evening when I pulled up in front of the store. I was about to get out of the car when I saw, for the first time, the logo on the side of the building: THE ORIGINAL HOME OF THE FAMOUS AMOS CHOCOLATE CHIP COOKIE. It seemed to be shining as if neon paint had been used. Or it was God lighting up my life at that moment. Anyway, I just sat in my car looking at the sign, not knowing anything special or profound to say, just sitting quietly, alone, embracing my moment of truth.

Then the rains came, creating havoc for the painters. I wasn't concerned, though: too much had gone on before this, so I remained optimistic. It was still raining when my sons Michael and Gregory and my longtime friend Chuck Fly arrived from New York. It was important to me that they be present at the opening, because my projections for the future included them and their being involved with the cookie business.

Finally the downpour, which had lasted all week, ended Saturday night, when I decided to do a little pouring myself. The cookies needed attention so that they would be at their best for our guests on Sunday. I was really looking forward to pouring all my ingredients into my large mixer. At home, I never used an electric mixer, just a large bowl, and I stirred the ingredients by hand, using a wooden spoon. I had to beat it fast, then in the final stages I had to really whip it up and cream it to get it just right. It was a lot of work, which made me very tired. But that was the way I did it when I made my homemade chocolate chip cookies at home.

Now I was in business making homemade cookies, and with a lot more help, in the form of equipment. I was the only one at the time who knew how to mix the cookies, so it was my job to create the first batch. The opening of my first case of pecans was a very special moment. When I bought pecans in the supermarket they were in small 2¾-ounce packs. Now I had a 30-pound case, and when I opened it I put my hands down into the pecans and let them trickle through my fingers like gold nuggets. What a great moment this was, having *all* of these pecans at my disposal.

So, after measuring everything out—with me happy as a lark, singing, having a good time, and totally in my glory—I mixed my batter in this 60-quart mixer bowl. After that I had to get the dough on my baker's tray. At home I did it with a teaspoon, which I had to do on this occasion as well. So there I was measuring out dough with a teaspoon, one cookie at a time, and placing them on this 18 × 27-inch baker's tray, which held, maybe, 120 cookies. Then it was placed on a rack until enough trays were accumulated to go into the oven.

This slow process went on all night. Friends would stop by to give me words of encouragement. Then, about 5 A.M., I stopped baking the butterscotch chip cookies with pecans, which I had started first, because the chocolate chip cookies with pecans were the product—the premium cookie—which everyone would be looking for. About 8 or 9 A.M. my people arrived at the shop, and after I instructed them in the baking of the cookies, I took my weary body—I had been going so long, I didn't know how tired my body was—to the nearest Jacuzzi and steam room to energize it.

I returned to the premiere and the opening of the Famous Amos Chocolate Chip Cookie store in Hollywood, Sunday, March 9, 1975, at about 1 P.M. Everyone I had invited, plus quite a few new Friends of The Cookie, had obviously decided to go ahead without me, because what I saw when I got back to the store were people everywhere having nonstop fun, having "a very brown day."

It was a great day and a great experience for me. I had accomplished something which I never stopped believing I would do. It just proved to me that when you have enough positive energy going for you good things will happen. Things only fail to happen when you doubt yourself and when you begin to draw back. I tell people all the time that the only reason my Hollywood store and Famous Amos happened was because I made a commitment. Once I had made the commitment, I went out and did it. You cannot be totally committed sometimes.

11

The universe always says yes.

We opened the Hollywood store that Monday, March 10, 1975—the day after the premiere party—at about 11 A.M., and people were already standing in lines outside of the store. As I had expected, word of mouth from our Sunday premiere had spread, and people were anxious to buy Famous Amos Chocolate Chip Cookies. It was to be the beginning of a wonderful but also extremely trying time.

First of all, I didn't have a cash register yet. I had paid for a used one, but I couldn't pick it up until later that day. Shirlee, my wife—although we were separated—was the cashier. I knew I needed somebody I could trust, and even though we weren't together, Shirlee and I were still friends. Also joining me on this maiden voyage was my right arm Ellen Cullum, who had been indispensable during the preparations for the opening; Jerry Gardner and his wife Carolyn: and Ruby, my mother. Each of them brought something special to the store for me: Ellen had been one of the builders of this landmark; Shirlee was someone I had been close to, and the mother of my youngest son, Shawn, who was one of the first to help me clean the store; Jerry and Carolyn had been close personal friends when I was in show business, and although they were late joining the Cookie Trip they were creative, devoted, hard workers; and Ruby, my indefatigable mother, kept Tony Christian's artistry spotless, as well as taking care of the plants and adding some herself. It was truly a family affair those first days of Famous Amos.

The staff, the setting, everything was perfect. I saw that original Hollywood store as the beginning of something special. It was a showcase for chocolate chip cookies, because I believed there were other people who loved chocolate chip cookies as much as I did. Now they had the opportunity to get more involved, eat more, and become more aware of chocolate chip cookies. However, in order for all I was perceiving to come out right, I had to get a full understanding of how to bake cookies with the equipment I had purchased.

One thing about baking cookies at home, you don't have large confusing equipment to master. You simply measure a small amount of the ingredients, mix them, place the batter on the cookie sheets, and bake them at the proper temperature. Well, as much as I wanted homemade cookies in my store, I couldn't do it the old way. I had to use more complicated equipment to make larger quantities. First, I had to figure out why the beater on the mixer fell off every time it stopped. I was fortunate that I had a salesman like Clarence Tucker, who immediately diagnosed that the wiring was simply reversed and, once corrected, I was able to move forward with our baking.

Another problem with my "homemade" habits, the kind which almost put me out of business, concerned the ingredients going into my cookies. I knew that the product I was turning out did not taste anything like the cookies I made at home. Then a telephone call came in from a friend of mine over at A&M Records, a girl named Julie, who said, almost whispering, "Wally, I don't know how to tell you this, but the cookies are not tasting the way they used to."

You can imagine what this did to me. Suddenly I was having wide-awake nightmares, thinking that any day I'd be out of business. I thanked Julie for her discretion in letting me know this. Even before Julie's call I had known there was something wrong with the cookies, which I was already trying to correct. Eventually I did, but it took a little while.

One other incident, which was quite embarrassing, took place when an elderly lady came into the store. She had just bought some cookies, and I watched her reach into the bag and pull one out to take a bite. This was not unusual for me to do; watching my customers bite into my cookies had always been one of my favorite pastimes. Well, it wasn't going to be a favorite this time, because when this lady took a bite she couldn't. She also looked as though her mouth had broken. I was embarrassed. I felt the need to defend The Cookie. So I took a sample and bit into it. I had the same experience. Once again the nightmares started up, a lot more frightening this time. I just knew that morning was close when I would wake up and everybody would be saying: "What's so good about Famous Amos cookies?"

About this same time I flashed back to a time soon after I began baking cookies at home. I was so proud and pleased with myself for having picked up where Aunt Della left me. So, one day after I baked a batch of cookies, I went to visit Ruby with some of these proudly prepared gems. My Grandma Julia was living with Ruby at the time, so I invited her to taste my efforts. I expected the praises to come instantly. Grandma Julia took a taste, and then a snarl came across her face. "Boy," she said, "these cookies got too much salt in them." My pride was shaken, and I disputed her accusation. I had been baking them all this time, and eating them day in and day out, so I knew better. Grandma Julia said she knew what she was talking about. Trying to prove her wrong, I tasted one of the cookies. I didn't want to believe it, but sure enough there was a salt taste. Too much salt will throw the flavor off. Just think, that eighty-five-year-old grandmother of mine still had her taste buds in tune. Me, I went back to correct my ingredients.

Finding the perfect recipe was constant trial and error for about a year, but I could sense the Cookie Trip was evolving, and it was evident that it was being developed by the people who worked for Famous Amos during that first year. However, we later developed a personnel problem. The turnover was great, mainly because the people who came in seeking work were mostly transients, and with transients you take on unreliability.

I had been brought up with a totally different work ethic than most of the people I was hiring. I was taught that even if I was doing something for nothing I should do it to the best of my ability. That's what I expected from the people who came to work for me: I expected them to have the same values as I. I also hoped that they would see the opportunities that success would bring, and the long-term financial rewards *after* the cookie business had worked. I was wrong. They could only deal with "What am I getting today?" and to hell with tomorrow. My problem, however, was that whatever I got each day—whatever money came in—had to be used to keep Famous Amos going, day to day. It was definitely hand-to-mouth.

In spite of my personnel woes, I still had to concern myself with keeping the "brown fever" going, which was continuing because of my publicity plan. It had worked to get everyone out for the premiere party, if only because they were curious. I sparked that curiosity with fliers and invitations, which I personally hand-delivered because I couldn't afford to mail them. This was what I'd done when I was a personal manager in show business. Now that I was in the cookie business managing The Cookie, my client could be whatever I wanted it to be—a rock show, a movie, or whatever—just as long as it was *fun.*

Fun to me was promoting The Cookie in the same way a movie is promoted and advertised: "coming attractions," "now playing," "coming soon," and "Wally Amos Presents." That's how I tied myself to the promotion. The star of this extravaganza was the chocolate chip cookie with pecans, with the other cookies being "guest stars." I also decided that I would not lack for critical comments about The Cookie and my own authorities about the cookie world. Therefore I created put-on quotes from "Van D. Camp" and "The Norman Tabernacle Choir," which were corruptions of names we are all familiar with. Clare Baren, Chuck Casell's wife, gave me a real quote when she said that eating the Butterscotch Chip Cookie was "Love at First Bite." Each of these put-ons and what-have-yous was just like Chuck Casell's "Brief History of the Chocolate

Chip Cookie," capable of creating a lot of curiosity, positive results, and *fun*.

I soon found that I would have to get physically involved with the fun I was creating on behalf of Famous Amos. Initially, there were magazine articles, television interviews, and the like soon after the Hollywood store opened. It finally got to the point when I was not only the promoter, I was the promotee. Therefore I had to resolve, "I am Famous Amos! If I don't promote The Cookie, who will?"

However, that grand decision was not without anxieties. First of all, I had never been in the spotlight. I was always in the background when handling my clients, but my new client was different: it was necessary for me to be out front, and I had no choice. Then I discovered I *was* entertaining. So I started projecting more of myself; I performed like I was onstage; you know, the delivery, the ideas. I was suddenly a total creative being. Why not? All the funny put-ons were from me and were my own concepts and creations. Also, if I didn't do it, it would never happen.

But becoming famous can be dangerous, especially if you're running a business. There are many people who want to take what you've put a lot of positive energy into and turn it into a negative experience. Soon after we had opened the Hollywood store, an incident that had the makings of a negative experience actually turned into an almost laughable situation.

I experienced my first robbery just as we were about to close one night. With me at the store was one of my employees, named Anita, who also lived close to me so I gave her a ride home if she worked late. Since I had to lock the front door of the store, and also pick up my clean laundry in the office, I told Anita to meet me in the rear parking lot. The laundry was mostly shirts, which Ruby had washed for me. That was her way of helping me save money, which it certainly did. Anyway, in the parking lot I started to get into my car, when all of a sudden a voice speaking from the other side of the wall said: "Awright, Amos, throw the bag across the wall."

My immediate reaction was that a friend of mine was playing a practical joke on me. I had many such friends, so it was possible. I didn't respond. The voice spoke again and made the same request, which was about the time I saw a gun pointing at me through a nearby hedge. So, without waiting to be asked a third time, I threw the bag of laundry over the wall and told Anita to get in the car, quick! I did the same and got the hell out of there. I notified the police when I got home and told them the entire story of what happened. My own thoughts turned to the robber, because I wondered what his reaction was when he opened the bag and saw only clean laundry. For some days after that incident I was afraid he might come back, unsatisfied with what he had gotten. Nothing happened, but that, unfortunately, was not the end of such attempts.

One of the best reasons *not* to try to rob me, at that time, was my scarcity of cash, because I was not making as much as I was spending. Where I did have credit, with my vendors, I was overextended. Then one day, Wesco, which was my primary supplier of flour, sugar, and all the basic ingredients, stopped the mule train, so to speak. I owed them more money than they were willing to extend credit for. All during the time we did business they gave me good service, and there was a loyalty between Wesco and Famous Amos. But all of a sudden their loyalty disappeared when I couldn't pay right away.

Because of my own loyalty to Wesco I would not deal with anyone else or listen to what they were offering. Then, suddenly, I had no choice. I had to do business with someone else. That turned out to be with a salesman named Bob Belton, of Continental Food Service. He had been a constant visitor to the store, trying to interest me in his supplies. I called Bob, saying I was "thinking" about using some of his supplies, and that we should start with margarine to see what kind of deal he would give me. Well, his deal was not bad at all. With Wesco I was buying 30-pound tubs of margarine, which required us to take the time to weigh the right amount for baking. Bob's company had margarine in one-pound cubes, which were a lot cleaner, quicker, and cheaper. Also, they were willing to extend me credit. So once again good came from what seemed to be a bad situation.

By August 1975 my income at the store still had not

picked up, but my publicity had. I was informed that a story
had allegedly run in the New York *Times* about Famous Amos,
which made me happy but curious. I didn't believe that our
popularity had reached back to the East Coast. Therefore I
checked with the New York *Times* to see if it was true, and it
was not. However, not too long after, a story was written and
was syndicated to other papers as well. That was the reason I
received a telephone call from Wes Gardner, the gourmet
buyer at Macy's in San Francisco. He had read about Famous
Amos and wanted to know if I would be interested in selling
cookies to Macy's. I was interested, but I wasn't set up to deal
with distribution anywhere but Los Angeles. So I told Wes,
"Hell, man, I'm trying my damnedest to sell cookies here!"
Also I wasn't set up to sell cookies wholesale. But it's funny
how Divine Order works, because some months before Macy's
called I had met Sid Ross, who was a coffee salesman then and
who would eventually get my wholesale business started. My
first dealings with Sid, though, didn't get started too well.

When I opened the Hollywood store I had planned to sell
milk and coffee along with my cookies. The coffee I was using
was a good strength, but I wanted Yuban, which I felt was a
quality coffee. One day Sid Ross came in with guarantees and
with 1½-ounce packs, which I could never get, so I gave him
the business. When I received my first order, there were
1¼-ounce packs, but I was charged for 1½-ounce packs, and I
was furious. I called Sid and bawled him out. He was apolo-
getic, because there had been an error, which he corrected.
From that moment on Sid and I had a great relationship—so
great he eventually joined Famous Amos.

Shortly after Macy's called, Sid came to me about helping
me establish the wholesale business. I was naturally curious
and definitely interested if it were possible. Sid had already
talked with Jurgensen's, a gourmet grocery company head-
quartered in Pasadena, California, which he felt looked like a
good prospect for getting a profitable wholesale contract. I had
problems, like cartons for a 300-pound order, proper ledgers,
and Jurgensen's policy of not paying for thirty days, which
wouldn't help my cash flow. Sid said he would do what was

necessary to set up my wholesale business. So a Volkswagen Rabbit I had acquired for deliveries, which I had decorataed with my trademarks and logo and a giant cookie on the hood, plus Sid's Pinto station wagon, made the first wholesale delivery to Jurgensen's. Later that same Rabbit would be the "commuter cookie" vehicle when I started doing business with Macy's, San Francisco. It also nearly became the quickest way to the poorhouse for me.

Maybe it was the color of the VW Rabbit, which was lemon yellow, because this car turned out to have more bugs in it than exposed garbage. Just about every time I took it in to be serviced, I came out with a bill and the promise that my problems were all over. Well, my problems, and my hopes for a broader wholesale business—as well as the Rabbit—almost went up in smoke when I was delivering my initial whosesale order to Macy's, because the car caught fire. I did manage to deliver the cookies to San Francisco, but I eventually got rid of the lemon-yellow VW Rabbit.

With my wholesale business under way, I was able to go out and drum up smaller wholesale locations. Establishing these new locations increased my cash flow, which I needed, and with Famous Amos Chocolate Chip Cookies being circulated to a wider audience, a greater amount of popularity evolved. One sign of this new popularity was an offer to open another Famous Amos store in a new shopping center in Studio City, California, right next to McDonald's. That was only the beginning, however, because I received another offer to take Famous Amos to Tarzana, California, in a shopping center called the Brown Center. Naturally, anything that complimented my "have a very brown day" interested me. Then, when I discovered that the people making the offer were named Vera and Gil Brown, I found it hard to refuse the natural kinship apparent in the request.

"You and this bag are entitled to be filled up at Famous Amos in Tarzana on August 17, 1975," was the way the invitation announcing the opening of the new store read. Like the Hollywood opening, it was a large party, and everyone brought those cookie bags, which had carried the invitations, to have them filled. This was an easier opening, for obvious reasons, and the first cookies baked at this new location were ceremoniously put into the oven by Vera Brown. She also got to take them out, and her first words when seeing them were, "Welcome to Tarzana, little cookies."

It was a generous welcome that first week, because we grossed $5,000. However, we gradually began to backslide, and we never picked up. For three years I stayed at the Tarzana location hoping something would happen, but nothing did. It was during this slow period that I received some good advice. There were three things to remember in selecting a retail site: "Location, location, location."

Shortly after the Tarzana store opening, when we were barely making a go of it, I received a call from a man named Bill Nelson, a business teacher in Tucson, Arizona, saying he wanted to open a store there. Bill's request was premature, considering what was going on—or not going on—in Tarzana. He understood and said he would keep in touch. That he did, and I got to like him because he had such a great sense of humor. That, plus his consistent keeping in touch with me, made me decide to stop off in Tucson on my return from a business trip to New York. When I finally met Bill Nelson, I also took a look at Tucson, and I decided that maybe it would not be a bad idea to put Famous Amos there.

It was my gut feeling and intuition which helped me make that decision, since I had not been exposed to the advice about "Location . . ." Anyway, I thought it was a good deal. Also I was encouraged to go ahead with this latest store by my business trip, which resulted in my reaching an agreement with Bloomingdale's to sell cookies in their store. So I felt maybe I was on an upswing. Actually, it was more like a pendulum, because I had promised to be in New York for Bloomingdale's to do some promotions on Saturday, May 8, 1976, with the opening-day party in Tucson on Sunday, May 9. I might have forgone the Tucson date if it had not been for the fact that I had to show everyone there how to mix the ingredients for the cookies.

The dates came, and I made my trip to New York and

managed to fulfill my commitment to Tucson. It was a successful opening day, with well over a thousand people turning out.
As was the case in Tarzana, the first week was great, but then
the backsliding began, and eventually this store had to close its
doors because of the lesson I later learned about opening a
retail store: "Location, location, location."

"You simply *must* be in Bloomingdale's!" was the demand
made by Barbara Dullien, a customer who later became a
friend, around November 1975. Barbara, who was a fashion
designer, was not making an unwarranted suggestion. As much
as I appreciated her feeling that I should be in Bloomingdale's,
with all that I was going through just trying to keep the Hollywood and Tarzana stores going, I thanked her, but I passed.

Later that same year, during December, Barbara came into
the store to buy cookies to give as Christmas presents to the
executives at Bloomingdale's. She was once again insistent
about my being in Bloomingdale's. This was a better time for
me, so I said maybe. Barbara suggested that I come to New
York in January 1976, when she would be introducing her fashion line, which I agreed to do. Before my arrival in New York,
I sent Marvin Traub, president of Bloomingdale's at the time,
my "Care" package, which included cookies, T-shirts, a poster,
and various other Famous Amos souvenirs, including my press
kit. I wanted Marvin to be familiar with me and The Cookie
when we arrived.

Identifying me as "someone" was not hard when I got to
Bloomingdale's, since I wore this very noticeable jump suit
with a cookie embroidered on the back. It was one of my more
important promotional tools and was capable of drawing attention, although it was not my intention to take the spotlight
from Barbara Dullien, who was having her line of clothes introduced. However, with all the attention I received, I only got
to meet Phil Kelly, who was vice-president of the department
Barbara was linked to. The next day I called Marvin Traub's
office to tell them I had sent my "Care" package, which they
acknowledged had arrived, and to say I was in town. I also let
them know I had to leave in a couple of days, and if Marvin
was interested in meeting with me, he should call before I left.

If he didn't, I would understand. Later that same day I got a call from Robert Gumport, the food buyer, saying that Marvin had asked him to contact me, and that I should come and meet with him. That meeting was between two haughty people; me, because I had all of this publicity and I felt I was very important, and Gumport, because he had been the major buyer and *the* connoisseur of gourmet foods at Bloomingdale's for over thirty years. So when I arrived his attitude was, "Just who does this guy think he is?" The first thing out of his mouth was: "I've tasted the cookies and I think they're too dry. I don't think they're so hot." My response was immediate and final: "Then you don't have to buy them," and I got up to leave. But Gumport stopped me and decided we should talk.

As I learned later, Gumport was only the first line of fire. He screened me first, then James Schoff, Jr., an executive vice-president, was called in. We went over the same things I had said to Gumport, who interjected several negative remarks from time to time. Finally I got tired of all of this and said, "Look, if you guys don't want the cookies, that's okay. You don't have to buy them. I'll just leave." Schoff stopped me, and we talked longer; enough so that when I left Bloomingdale's I had a deal to sell Famous Amos cookies there. Now my problems really began.

I wasn't yet baking cookies on the East Coast. I thought about shipping them from Los Angeles to New York, but I considered how costly that would be and ruled it out. Therefore I made the decision to open up a bakery on the East Coast in time to fulfill my promised delivery date for our first order, which was June 9, 1976. I was not worried about my promise, because I still had Chuck Fly, whom I could call upon, to run the East Coast operation. Also there was the universe, which I had a feeling was going to say yes to me again.

When Sid Ross first entered my Hollywood store that September of 1975, the universe had said yes to me, although I would not realize it until later, in 1976, when Sid joined the Famous Amos family. The fact is, he was anxious to be a part of my thriving business. He even worked five months with no salary, because he could see the potential in Famous Amos, and

was turned on enough to loan us money. He was that committed, and I, in turn, felt committed to him. Also Sid became a
challenge for me, as you will see later in this chapter. But,
suffice to say, Sid evolved into an incredible person after joining me in my businesss, and he's gone through an absolute
transformation.

When I first met Sid he was this brash young guy who
would do anything to sell his product. He smoked cigars, drove
a big Cadillac, and had a house in the fashionable Granada
Hills section, where he lived with his wife Claudia and their
two children, Darren and Danny. Sid was also paranoid and
wanted to control everything. Delegating authority was not one
of his strong suits. But, with all of those faults, he was a hard
worker. He knew the wholesale business very well, and he did a
great job keeping my retail stores—in Hollywood and Tucson—
going in a solid way. That's why, when I needed to go to the
East Coast to set up our new Famous Amos commissary to supply Bloomingdale's with cookies, I knew that my new head of
the West Coast operations, Sid Ross, could handle it.

I returned to New York in February 1976, ready to start an
East Coast operation but without the money to do so. Prior to
my arrival, Chuck Fly, who would run the operation on the
East Coast, had already tried looking for locations but had no
luck. Immediately, upon my arrival, I pitched in by going
through newspapers and telephone books until I reached a real
estate agency in New Jersey and an agent named Pat Sullivan.
When I told Pat what I was looking for, he told me about a
place that turned out to be too large, but he also knew someone with a smaller one which we could sublet if we liked it.
Chuck and I decided to look at it. Why not? We had nothing
to lose.

Chuck and I met Pat Sullivan at a Howard Johnson's on
Route 3, where he picked us up to drive to the location of the
building—in Nutley, New Jersey. When he told us the city we
were going to, I said, "You must be kidding!" But he wasn't. I
suddenly became excited, but at the same time I just knew that
this was going to be *the* place. When we got to the building
there was no doubt. Questions started forming in my mind:

Why did the first place I saw turn out to be the right one? Also, in a town called Nutley? Divine Order. The more these kinds of things happened, the more I developed a stronger faith, a stronger belief in a Supreme Being and a divine energy in the universe. Whatever it was, I felt strongly that it had brought me to Nutley, New Jersey, where I signed a lease for a building which would establish Famous Amos on the East Coast.

There was still the need for money, however. A lot of equipment was needed. A single oven would cost $25,000, as much as the entire budget to open my Hollywood store. The required budget was sizable, and I couldn't get it from a bank because I had no collateral. All that I had was the name Famous Amos, which only I, unfortunately, thought was worth gold. Also about this same time I had the Tucson store on the drawing board, and money was needed for that. The problem was that, unlike the normal businessman, I did not sit down to do a projection of budgets and costs before going ahead with it. I did it the only way I knew—ass backward. But there was a reason: I was from a show business background, so I was used to "flying by the seat of my pants."

I found a way to pay for the oven, through Bloomingdale's. They arranged for me to get it, and I would pay them back by subtracting a portion of the money from invoices due Famous Amos from Bloomingdale's. As for the other money, I decided I would accomplish what I needed to with money made at my other locations. Also, if it was necessary I would write checks, whether I had the money or not. This was not the best way; it was the *only* way to solve my Nutley financial needs. However, another monkey wrench had been thrown into my hopes of getting Nutley going: the building I leased was not zoned for a bakery.

Funny, there was a doughnut shop and restaurant one block down the street, but the location I was leasing was not in that zone. Where we were was all right for coal trucks and industrial things that would produce smog and dirt. A garbage dump could have been placed there, but not a bakery. Eventually we had to go before the City Council with our zoning

problem. It finally got to a point where one of the Councilmen
got tired and bored with the bureaucracy and pointed out,
"What we're doing here doesn't make sense. Here's a man talking about bringing income into the community, employment,
and a reputable name. He's even going to make the area smell
good. What are we arguing about? Let's just approve the rezon-
ing." So they did.

Because of the Nutley zoning problem we were not able to
meet our delivery date to Bloomingdale's, although I had that
covered. We made the delivery of cookies for opening day by
airmailing them in from Tucson and Los Angeles. So the
opening was just as auspicious as any I had had before. The
Cookie was still the center of attraction, placed on a satin pil-
low on a pedestal in the front of the boardroom at Bloomingdale's, where we held a press conference. However, while the
500 pounds of airmailed cookies were being sold I slipped away
to find out if I was going to be able to cover the $15,000 I had
overwritten in our checking account.

I met with Stu Brown, an investment analyst I had met in
Los Angeles and become friends with before my contract with
Bloomingdale's. Stu, who is very sharp and consistent in his
thinking and ideas, went right to work to find me lenders.
These lenders were a saving grace, and by helping me move
ahead with Nutley, they helped Famous Amos become more famous.

Doing business with Bloomingdale's was instrumental in
increasing our wholesale business. Unfortunately, our eastern
operation under Chuck Fly's direction was not going the way I
had hoped it would. It soon became clear to me that Chuck's
previous career had not prepared him for what I was asking
him to do. He was, first of all, a stand-up comedian. He had
also been in record promotion and eventually had become my
associate in my personal management business. He had never
run a business producing a product, nor had he handled payroll
or large numbers of employees. He was a good friend, but he
wasn't qualified. What I needed was someone with business
savvy, whether he was a friend or not. Chuck did not have

what was needed to do the job that was needed. Later I would come to the same conclusion about myself.

For a while I left Chuck alone, but that became costly in terms of personnel morale and employee relations. Therefore I decided to bring in some assistance for Chuck—another friend of mine from my show business days, John Rosica. One thing about Rosica, his background was in administration, which he had gotten from being an executive in the recording business. Prior to my calling on Rosica to work at Nutley, he and his wife Marilyn made an effort to get my mail-order operation going in a fluid way. They paid for advertising in various publications, but nothing major came of it. About this same time Rosica began spending a lot of time at Nutley, so I got him more involved with the operation.

I thought my idea was feasible. I wanted to ease Rosica into the Nutley operation, thus freeing Chuck so he could get out on the road making sales and generating more business. Rosica's presence made Chuck feel slighted, although Chuck's feeling was premature because I suddenly found that Rosica was also miscast. Looking back, I realize I was wrong not to terminate both of them, but I waited, since I was now making plans to move to Hawaii.

I did make a pair of terminations, my first and most difficult. As I mentioned earlier, Shirlee was my original cashier when the Hollywood shop opened. Eventually she became a problem, especially when any woman who knew me came into the shop. She would become hostile, although I'm not sure she realized what she was doing. It may have been a subconscious reaction, but it happened once too often. Also the business was growing, and I couldn't handle personal and domestic problems as well as business decisions. So I asked Shirlee to leave the business. I didn't have the guts to tell her in person, though, so I did it by calling her on the telephone.

My other painful termination was my mother. Ruby's problem was her desire to be manager of the Hollywood shop. There was also her feeling about protecting her son's business, which sometimes made her rather unkind. She would compare other people to me, and if they didn't work as hard as I had starting the business, then they had to deal with Ruby. That meant she would swing brooms and even threaten to throw hot water on them. I couldn't let that go on, so I was forced to terminate Ruby, which I did with a letter.

As it turned out, Shirlee's hostility toward other women, because of their interest in me, was unnecessary. I was not interested in those or any other women from October 1974, when I began planning the Cookie Trip, until long after the Hollywood store opened in March 1975. I was just too committed to making the cookie business work. If there was a hint of a relationship with any woman, that's all it was. There was no telling what I might have become had I not had this unusual meeting with Christine.

"My friends say my chocolate chip cookies are better than yours," a flight attendant said when I was boarding an airplane for a return flight from New York to Los Angeles. It was in July 1976, and I had Shawn with me. The comment caught me off guard, but I smiled, nodded, and said, "Fine, I accept that." Then we went to our seats. Thinking about the incident, I decided it was okay with me if someone disliked my cookies, so I thought no more about the comment, or the person who had made it.

Some time later, after we were in flight, this same flight attendant came back to our seats with ice cream for me and Shawn, and some additional comments about her cookies versus mine. Since Shawn and I were enjoying the ice cream it was hard to bite the hand feeding us. However, ice cream was little compensation when someone was putting down my labor of love.

In time the conversation took another direction, which included finding out that my cookie assailant's name was Christine Harris, and that her labor of love, when not a flight attendant for TWA, was art. She lived in New York City, which was her home base, but Los Angeles was one of her regular trips. Art was her hobby, and when she showed me pictures of some of her work, which she called "fabric painting," it was unique, and perfect for an idea I had with regard to Famous Amos promotions. Since I had been wearing my jump suit with the large cookie on the back so much, I had been thinking of putting the logo on a jacket as well. Christine's fabric painting would serve that purpose very well. Therefore I told her I might want to commission her at a later date, and she gave me her card.

Waiting outside the terminal in Los Angeles, I saw the golden hair of a flight attendant go past me to a waiting car, and she turned out to be Christine. I decided I didn't want her to get away before I gave her my card, so I went to catch her. I suggested that, since she flew in and out of Los Angeles a lot, she should give me a call on one of her trips, and "I'll treat you to some cookies and milk at my store in Hollywood." The comment drew a chuckle because it probably sounded like a line to pick up women. I gave her my business card at the same time I made the offer, but before I could get a yes or no, Christine had to leave.

Nothing happened after that encounter and offer, and I didn't make any attempts to contact her, although I did think about her often. Then, around September 1976, I had to go on a promotional trip to Detroit, then on to New York. I got the jacket and mailed it to Christine with a note telling her when I would be in New York, which wouldn't be too soon for me since I was *really* anxious to see her again. That meeting, however, would be preceded by my trip to Detroit and promotions at Hudson's, a department store that carried the cookies.

When I finally got to New York, my first telephone call was to Christine, and I was lucky to catch her. It seemed she had just gotten in, because she could not get a return flight out of Los Angeles, and so she had to go to San Francisco in order to get a plane which would put her back in New York in time to see me. Divine Order, which I was not cognizant of at the time, was working to make this meeting take place. Since I was so anxious to see her, I suggested we have dinner somewhere. Christine countered with having dinner at her apartment, which I did not refuse. Since she had a car, she said she would pick me up at my hotel.

At 6:30 P.M. I came through the hotel doors just as she pulled up in her white Toyota station wagon. I had thought many times about what our next meeting would be like, but at this moment I was just happy and pleased that it was finally taking place. Then when I got into her car I was given an unusual gift: a bowl of her freshly baked and still warm chocolate chip cookies, which were sitting on some aluminum foil that was covering some ice surrounding a split of champagne with a green ribbon around the neck. I was pleased and surprised at the unusual gift, which was topped off with Christine's smile and "Welcome to New York."

Christine's apartment was an extension of her art and very much reflected her own personality. It had artifacts, color, and her fabric paintings, which I thought were just fantastic and most unusual, all of which contributed to its happiness and friendliness.

After we ate a portion of the Chinese food we had picked up, I started talking nonstop in an effort to make up for the lost time of not seeing her. I also asked why she had not accepted my invitation to join me for cookies and milk.

"I thought you were like all the other guys, trying to get attention," Christine explained. "I said to myself, 'So he sells cookies. Who does he think he is anyway? I make better cookies than his.' That's when I decided to throw your business card away."

I liked Christine's honesty, which I had experienced when we first met, and the fact that who I was made no difference to her. At that moment, nothing but Christine made any difference to me. Maybe it was love, or her honesty, or the feeling of being so relaxed while I was with her. Whatever it was, I enjoyed it and Christine for at least three hours before I was compelled to kiss her. When I did it lasted almost as long as it took for me to do it. Christine wondered why it took me so long. I didn't have an answer. Maybe it was because I was out of practice, or afraid of being rejected, or maybe I was afraid that kissing her would be a commitment I would have to make to this woman, something I had not done in a long time. Whatever it was, I put it behind me and proceeded to kiss

Christine again; this time nonstop, and into the night, thus consummating and commencing our relationship.

Something had happened, to both Christine and to me, but I don't think it was love. We decided we wanted to be together, which meant no outside interference, either from the guy she had been seeing, or from her job, or from my cookie business. She also understood that marriage was out for me. The fact that I even considered putting my cookie business on hold was odd for me, since my reason for coming to New York had been to promote The Cookie and the business. I did not, however, make myself totally unavailable, because I did make daily calls to my operation in Los Angeles and told them where I could be contacted, which was now at Christine's apartment. Well, one evening a call from an old friend named Nancy Brown brightened my day when she asked me, "How would you like to come to Hawaii?"

It was a strange offer. "For years," I said, "since my military days there, I haven't wanted to do anything else. If I can sell Famous Amos Chocolate Chip Cookies there, of course I want to come to Hawaii." Well, that's exactly what Nancy's call was all about. It seemed Nancy, whom I had first met when I was doing a Macy's promotion in San Francisco, was now a buyer for McInerny's, one of the larger specialty stores in Hawaii. Her boss, Stan Ueyama, merchandising manager for the store, had brought up Famous Amos at a buyers' meeting, saying that we were the hottest item in the mainland department stores. Thus plans were made for me to travel to Hawaii in February 1977. With that piece of news, it was time for me to get back to work, since I had overstayed my time on the East Coast. But I would work my way back to Los Angeles, with a slight vacation with Christine, who had taken some time off.

After a brief stop in Detroit we continued on to San Francisco, but we first stopped at Big Sur. This was a perfect place for us lovebirds—or for any lovebirds—because of its beautiful sunsets, casual walks on the beach, and cuddling by the fireplace during the evening chill. We both fell in love with the location, and I made the suggestion that it would not be a bad place to move to permanently. The way I felt about Christine, I would have been willing to live anywhere with her, and especially Big Sur. However, the cookie business needed me, and we shortened our trip in order for me to get back to the business of making and selling chocolate chip cookies.

Shortly after Christine and I arrived in Los Angeles it was time for her to go back to New York. This was unpleasant for both of us, and the time when I would see and be with her again seemed a long way off. Therefore I proposed that Christine get a transfer. She doubted she could, but when she asked it was granted. So I made another trip to New York in January to move Christine to Los Angeles, after which we would go to Hawaii to begin selling cookies. We decided to drive cross-country in her Toyota, which proved to be a bad idea since we ran into the worst winter (1977) the Midwest had seen in years. To escape the icy roads, we stopped off briefly in Cleveland, Ohio, to recharge our nerves and to see an old friend of mine from Los Angeles, a disk jockey named Lee "Baby" Simms.

Lee had dropped into my life about the same time I was trying to get Famous Amos into the mouths of many. It was Lee's gift of gab, so to speak, on radio station KRLA that got us together, especially when he made the announcement that he was going to leave Los Angeles if he didn't get some chocolate chip cookies. The ironic thing was I didn't know Lee at the time, but we soon met, became friends, and eventually started a routine on radio which was a great help in promoting my cookies and developing our friendship. The business about leaving L.A. unless he got some chocolate chip cookies was just one of the many "trips" Lee would take an audience on, including me. I primarily became tripped out over how creatively funny he was, and still is.

As planned, I went to Hawaii in February 1977 to sell cookies at McInerny's, which was located in the Ala Moana Shopping Center. There was some trepidation on my part, because I wasn't sure how Famous Amos would be received. However, I put that all behind me because the promotion arrangements were so much different than any other I had done.

For one thing, our accommodations were first class, with a suite on the twenty-first floor of the Hilton Hawaiian Village in Waikiki, with full view of the ocean and harbor.

McInerny's had also surprised me by getting the media to come to me at the hotel, something that was definitely different from other promotions. It prompted me to recall and comment, "My God, I never managed an act that had the media come to the hotel for interviews." It all felt good, and I felt more famous than any performer I had ever managed.

Everything went so well, the ten days I was scheduled to stay in Hawaii were extended to three weeks. Christine and I made excellent use of that time with our explorations to one other Hawaiian island, Maui. It was also during that time that we made the decision to move to Hawaii permanently. That was an easy one because of the beautiful weather, clear days, excellent beaches, and the warm and friendly aloha spirit of the people. Aloha is the official Hawaiian greeting and farewell. To express aloha is also to give love. The only other thing I had to do was pave the way for a new cookie shop, which Stan Ueyama, who had brought me to Hawaii, said he could help me with. Convincing my associates that my move was a good idea was not so easy. They felt I would be "so far away." So I pointed out to them that Hawaii would be just an airplane ride to any promotions, and I certainly wasn't planning to stop promoting The Cookie.

Bloomingdale's, however, was going to stop selling Famous Amos cookies, which I learned about when I returned from Hawaii. Actually, in October 1976, our exclusive contract with Bloomingdale's—which was for a year—came up for discussion. This was because Macy's in New York approached me about selling cookies in the new Cellar boutique they were opening. So, with our exclusivity now coming to an end, we approached Bloomingdale's with the idea of selling to both stores, which they did not approve. Therefore we discontinued selling at Bloomingdale's and began selling cookies at Macy's in New York in June 1977. It turned out that we sold more cookies, wholesale, than we had at Bloomingdale's, and it also gave me the opportunity to become a part of the great Macy's Thanksgiving Parade.

Being with Bloomingdale's, we received a lot of prestige and recognition. But the Macy's parade placed Famous Amos in the home of at least 20,000,000 television viewers. That was a lot of promotion for just one sitting; which, in reality, turned out to be four sittings—1977, 1978, 1979, 1980—four years in a row. I was also pleased about being in the Macy's parade for personal reasons. I had seen this same parade as a kid, and when I became a parent I took my own kids. The other important part of the Macy's parade is the prestige you receive by being in it; the kind of prestige that is on a par with being on the cover of *Time* magazine (which I was), and being in the Smithsonian Institution (which I am). Also the Macy's parades are put on with fantastic enthusiasm by the employees from all of the Macy's stores—from San Francisco, Kansas City, Missouri, and New York City. But Macy's greatest contribution takes place after the parade—about a week after—and doesn't get the same fanfare, although Macy's is to be praised for doing it.

Their Christmas party for underprivileged children, which I had the pleasure of hosting a couple of times, is replete with clowns, music, and refreshments. Each child also receives ten dollars to buy the gift of his or her choice. But if the gift costs more than the ten dollars, Macy's makes up the difference. Now that's a special kind of sharing with the community—a giving back to the community that supports you—which has to be appreciated. I do. I appreciate it very much.

About the spring of 1977, just before I moved to Hawaii, Famous Amos began to move, not only forward, but up, up, and away. Thanks to the media, Famous Amos became known as the cookie of the jet set. I had to agree with the labeling because we were reaching further and wider than ever before, thanks to our wholesale operation, and most assuredly our important new account, Neiman-Marcus, was jet set.

We got into that exclusive department store because of Edythe Scherer, her husband Martin, and their daughter, Sandy, as well as her husband, Richard Golber. They had ap-

proached me about licensing, manufacturing, and selling jewelry for Famous Amos, which was eventually introduced at
Bloomingdale's. Then, when they met Marty Hackel, merchandising manager for Neiman-Marcus, they were able to convince
him to bring Famous Amos to the nationally prominent department store. Selling cookies there prompted me to do promotions at their stores in Atlanta, Houston, and Dallas, but it
was the Dallas store's promotion that was special.

The promotion consisted of me and The Cookie arriving
on a Brink's armored truck. In this case, I rode in on the running board of the Brink's truck. Then, at the entrance to Neiman-Marcus, the guard, with his hand firmly on his gun, re-
moved the cookies, which were in silver bags, and carried them
into the store—still with his hand on his weapon—and placed
these precious morsels in a roped-off window area where a Famous Amos Boutique had been set up, the highlight of which
was our logo in neon. It was a unique and classy promotion
which everyone enjoyed, me in particular. After all, not too
long ago I had been a little black boy named Wallace Amos,
Jr., of Tallahassee, Florida, and I was now part of Neiman-
Marcus, the most prestigious department store in the United
States. I was also Famous Amos, the kazoo-blowing, happy-go-
lucky greeter of the Friends of The Cookie, a role I enjoy
playing. No matter how sophisticated the situation, people see
me as *fun* and want to have fun with me. I've been told that
seeing me makes them happy—a relief to them. I'm not pa-
tronizing, nor do I try to get anything out of the Friends of
The Cookie but a laugh. Being happy and blowing my kazoo is
all part of making that happen.

The kazoo as a part of my promotion and image was something that happened accidentally. One day I was making a delivery with my son Shawn to a shop called Propinquity. They
were selling gold-plated kazoos, which I had not seen in a long
time, and which I always thought of as fun musical instruments even though some people refer to them as toys. I decided I had to have one of those kazoos, so I made a trade with
the owner of the shop, which turned out to be a couple of bags
of cookies for a couple of kazoos for Shawn and me. We imme-

diately started playing them and went off happily on our kazoo-
blowing way. Shawn and I had so much fun, I decided to carry
that same fun into my Famous Amos promotions, so I made
the kazoo the official instrument of The Cookie; no other
cookie can lay claim to having its own instrument.

As we got closer to moving to Hawaii I spent as much
time with Shawn as possible, because he was taking the move
badly. That was natural because Shawn and I spent a lot of
time together, even though I did not live with him. During the
week I took him to school every morning, picked him up from
school most of the time, and spent every weekend with him
when I was in town. My move to Hawaii would cancel all of
that. So this was no mere temporary separation, like when I
went off on promotional or business trips. There would be
twenty-five hundred miles of water separating us. Worst of all
was Shawn's feeling that Christine was taking me away from
him.

In the past, I had carefully considered the feelings of my
sons when I separated from their respective mothers. I always
made it clear to them that no matter where I went, or who I
was with, I was still their father; that I was available if they
ever needed me, and that I loved them. Shawn didn't accept
this as well as his older brothers had, probably because Shawn
was older than they had been. Also possibly contributing to his
feelings of resentment for Christine was the fact that we were
not married—only living together. I tried reasoning with Shawn
by telling him he now had two homes, one in Los Angeles and
one in Hawaii. Also I told him I would be but a telephone call
away, day or night, and that a telephone would be installed in
his room for that purpose. None of this left Shawn very elated,
but he did, reluctantly, eventually accept my move.

On May 24, 1977, Christine and I said *Vaya con Dios* to
Los Angeles and, five hours later, *Aloha!* to Hawaii. Nancy
Brown, who was in part responsible for this move, met us at
the airport. She then took us to pick up our new car, which had
been shipped ahead. We went to the Kahala Hilton Hotel,
where we stayed for two weeks, while Mel Lum, a realtor who
had contacted me when he heard I was moving to Hawaii, tried

to find a place for us to live. Actually, Mel's call to me in Los Angeles was about locating a spot for a Famous Amos store. So, at the same time, it was decided he should find a residence for me and Christine. I was also planning ahead for the arrival of my three sons for the summer, so I had requested he find a large enough place to house all of us comfortably. Well, Mel Lum found the perfect spot—why not, everything else was working out so well—in an area called Hawaii Kai, which was a relatively new development outside of Honolulu. It was a condominium called the Esplanade, which was certainly large enough. It was the sunken bathtub, though, which convinced Christine and me that we had to make this our new home. Without a doubt, everything was in Divine Order.

On the mainland, some things changed, and I hoped it was for the best. The Nutley situation had not gotten any better with Chuck Fly and John Rosica at the helm. I had left it alone, and Chuck in particular, hoping he would find within himself a way to continue with Nutley, but that didn't happen either. So I decided to take my chances with John Rosica and see what came from his running the Nutley operation. Therefore I notified Chuck of his termination by telegram from Hawaii, and I hoped he would understand. He did, but with great reluctance. Chuck decided to seek a lawyer, complaining that his rights were violated, and threatened to take me to court. I simply told Chuck that I had the right to terminate his employment if I thought that was best for the company. I was sorry I had to do that, and my decision was not personal. In my opinion, it was simply the best thing for Famous Amos.

My first summer as a resident in Hawaii, 1977, could not have been better, especially with Christine, Michael, Gregory, and Shawn to share it with me. Even Shawn's reluctance to accept Christine did not bother me. It was an opportunity for me to take a good look at Michael and Gregory who, to my amazement, were now grown in many ways. They had arrived at that point where their lives were expanding, and there were other things they wanted to do now by themselves. They each had new friends, and girls were definitely on their minds, which meant my being around would not be as important as it used to be. Then I realized that Shawn would also be undergoing the same changes one day; and that one day he would better understand my being away from him with Christine. Time, I felt, would tell the entire story. So, after that wonderful summer, Christine and I settled down and worked on having a nice life in Hawaii. I also worked on getting the first Famous Amos store in Honolulu, with Christine right there with me, contributing in every way.

Meanwhile, the Van Nuys commissary was finally put together and began operating in July 1977. Sid Ross was in charge of running the new commissary, as well as being in charge of the West Coast. John Rosica was in charge of the East Coast, and I would be supervising the entire business from Hawaii, or so I thought. However, setting up the business in Van Nuys had been a strain, with Sid Ross carrying the brunt of it. Sid's problems, though, were not only at Famous Amos but at home.

Before I knew it, Sid and his wife had gotten a divorce. I knew there were business pressures, but I couldn't believe they were so bad that it would end his marriage. I was right; it wasn't the business. Sid discovered he was gay, which affected him terribly. Not only did he have to share this discovery with his wife, he had two kids whom he loved. He was worried about what they were going to say; what everybody was going to think, including me. But, through it all, Sid never said a word to me about his situation, although I knew he was under some pressure. It was, actually, Christine who finally learned of his being gay; then I heard, and I had a long talk with Sid. During that talk I made it unequivocally clear that I didn't care what he was. It didn't matter. In my eyes everybody was a child of God; everybody was a human being. My only concern was his performance with Famous Amos which, up until he discovered he was gay, was great. So all that mattered to me was that he be able to continue doing a great job for Famous Amos and find happiness for himself.

After that talk, with things getting out into the open, we

went back to business as usual; but there was some residual paranoia. Sid felt everybody was trying to get his job; he felt there was some undermining going on. He became very secretive and would not share information with other employees, which was almost too much for me to tolerate. But somewhere in all this was a lesson to be learned. Maybe I had not communicated it as well as I tried to live it, but I had always seen Famous Amos as an opportunity for people to express themselves; to be creative and to get out of life what they wanted out of it. That's what Famous Amos had given me; it had provided me that kind of opportunity. I wanted the other people working with me to realize the same opportunities, because they were there. Somehow that fact wasn't coming across, and certainly wasn't loud and clear.

But once again time took care of everything. Once I started attending Unity Church I was able to get Sid involved. Whenever I was in Los Angeles, Sid attended church with me. I also talked to him often and sent him inspirational things to read. Very slowly I could see Sid's personality begin to change; his being gay became less of a problem, became something he was willing to live with. He also began to care more about himself and less about whether someone liked him or not because he was gay. Sid even wrote an article for the gay magazine the *Advocate*, letting everybody know that he was gay and that Famous Amos also knew but that it didn't matter; that Famous Amos was a people business, and whatever kind of people happened to come along, if they did a good job there was a place for them in the company.

Sid had interpreted my feelings to the letter, and I was pleased by that. I was also pleased by his transformation, which had been tremendous, both mentally and physically. One thing which was affected was his nervous system, which created a condition called alopecia, and he lost his once full head of hair. But through all of that, and the stress which took its toll on Sid, he developed into a fantastic human being and a better leader. I felt good about Sid because I had opted to stick it out with him and let things take their proper course. When it was all over I made an important decision: I made Sid Ross presi-

dent of Famous Amos. I decided to let him run the company
on a day-to-day basis without interference from me. That was
something he could not have done before, although he was
probably the best person for the job. What he eventually went
through, I feel, truly made Sid Ross the right person for the job
of keeping the cookie business very brown. He also afforded me
the opportunity to learn some very important lessons.

After a year of togetherness in Hawaii, Christine and I
were still very happy. There were moments when Christine
would bring up marriage, but I would not commit to it. I was
still marriage-shy; two attempts had failed, and I wasn't prepared to hurt anyone else because I wasn't ready and because I
was still unsettled. There was also still some playing left in me,
and there were things I needed to get out of my system. Pretty
soon Christine realized this too, and in July 1978 we agreed to
separate. Shortly after that I went to New York on a business
trip, where I met a girl named Carol Denmark. It was a casual
acquaintance, nothing planned or intended. We became good
friends, pals, and then when I had to go on a promotional tour
she went with me. Then, upon my return to Hawaii, Carol
came along, and we lived together. Funny thing, though, Christine was never out of my mind; there was a kind of bond, or
something, that we had between us. From time to time I
would see Christine in passing, and I would try to help her in
any way I could, since she didn't know many people in Hawaii.
Like Christine, Carol was a great lady, but I was never totally
comfortable or absolutely happy with her.

In August 1978, when Carol and I returned to Hawaii
from the mainland promotional tour, the first thing she wanted
to do was go to church. I was somewhat reluctant, but not because I was an agnostic. I'd been raised in the Church, and as a
child I knew all the books in the Bible. I had always gone to
church on Sunday, whether it was with Aunt Della or Ruby.
Then, when I found I could not relate anymore, I drifted away.
I did believe, however, that there was a Supreme Being; that
there was some force keeping the universe together and making

it all work. I also knew there was much more to the world than what I was able to see. But I didn't believe I needed to go to church to see it, and I still don't. So, when Carol asked me to attend church with her, I refused. But Carol was insistent, and sold on Unity Church. She also felt that Unity was what I needed, and she said, "If you just go this one Sunday, then I won't ever ask you again."

After I went, Carol never had to ask me again. Unity confirmed my feelings that you don't have to worship a building, edifice, or a person, or anything. God is within, truly. You can deal with that whether you're in a church, in a store, on a beach, or anywhere. You can have church anywhere! So, realizing that, I started going to Unity with and without Carol. I found I was able to examine myself. I also became more honest with myself, and I realized that I should get what I wanted out of life. Most of all, that would have to be someone who really loved and cared about me, someone who was always in my corner and looking out for my best interest. Once I knew all of that, I realized the person I was needing was Christine, and I decided I wanted her back with me.

It was inevitable that the relationship between Carol and me would not last, because I did not find in Carol what I knew for certain was in Christine. Carol, however, had my respect for having brought me to Unity, which helped me to find myself. Shortly after Carol was gone, I called Christine to ask if we could meet and talk, and she agreed. I told her that we should get back together and give ourselves another try because I really did love her. It was my feeling that if we both concentrated at making our relationship work there was no reason it would not. Christine agreed, just as she agreed to attend Unity with me, and then that became a part of our togetherness.

Our next move was to find somewhere to live together, which we decided should be a house and not an apartment. We found a nice home in the quiet and peaceful section of Oahu called Lanikai. The sharing of that new home, however, would have to wait, because I had to go on an immediate promotional trip to the mainland. We were introducing chocolate chip cookies with macadamia nuts, inspired by Hawaii and

Christine's father, Frank Harris, who loved the nuts. Christine, meanwhile, managed to get us settled in our new love nest, which I could hardly wait to return to.

Marriage, and the discussion of marriage, had been prohibited in my life and my relationship with Christine. But now I felt that I was ready to face that decision one more time. It was during the promotional tour that I made the decision to ask Christine to marry me, but I delayed asking her because it was such a special moment for me, and for Christine, that I felt when I proposed I should do something extra.

When I visited Unity Village in Lee Summit, Missouri, while in Kansas City for a promotion with Macy's, I had made up my mind what I would do. At the Unity Village bookstore I bought a birthday book, which had a unique message, for Christine's birthday, which was in a couple of weeks. It was my intention to mail the book several days prior to her birthday— for arrival on that day—and include my proposal of marriage, which would be written in it. I was very pleased with how this different proposal would affect Christine. I was not pleased at all, however, with the news that reached me when I arrived in Pittsburgh, a stop on my promotional tour.

It was on Thursday, April 5, 1979, in Pittsburgh, the city of champions and steel mills, that I was told by John Rosica that my champion of inspiration, and one of the steel supports of The Famous Amos Chocolate Chip Cookie, might be dead. It seemed that unconfirmed reports were that Chuck Casell had committed suicide, which Rosica was going to check on. My immediate reaction was one of confusion, and I didn't want to believe it was true. So I immediately worked at erasing from my mind any images of Chuck being dead.

I was set up to do some interviews on television and on radio, with the first one on television. I was finding it difficult to be what I usually am known to be, and it was a struggle to get to the end of the interview. I was thinking only about what John would have to tell me when I saw him. Then, when I did see him, his face told me what I didn't want to accept. I had to, though, and I did it by standing alone and crying uncontrollably. I couldn't help it; Chuck and I were extremely close;

I actually felt a part of me had also died. Shawn, who was with me, saw and felt my emotions, and told me that I should not cry, and everything would work out for the best.

My radio interview was done, but it was a zombie doing it, only because I was trying to uphold the "show must go on" tradition. The disk jockey interviewing me knew what had happened, and we carried on. I, however, found it difficult to get through certain things which Chuck had done, like "A Brief History of the Chocolate Chip Cookie," because they brought back memories and prevented me from holding back the tears swelling up inside of me. I cried for a while before I reached any kind of composure. I needed to talk to someone, so I called Michael Murphy, my minister at Unity Church in Hawaii. It was the first time in my life I ever felt the need to make such a call. Michael was very reassuring and told me how life was eternal, with no beginning or end, and that Chuck had simply completed another phase of his life. His words had a calming effect on me. Later that night I called Christine, who also knew Chuck and understood how close we had been. Christine, whom I felt so close to, was perfect to help me out of my despair. So I decided to take out the birthday book, which I hadn't mailed yet, and read it to her—including the proposal of marriage. After I was finished reading, I formally asked Christine to marry me.

In making the proposal I said some things that needed to be said, both for my benefit and for Christine's. I told her my proposal was not without commitment; that I was now able to make such a commitment and that I was also able to withstand any pressures, or whatever was necessary to make our marriage work. Finally I admitted that this was the first time I had ever consciously made such a commitment to a woman, which touched Christine, as did everything I had said, and she accepted my proposal of marriage. We then decided that since I, ostensibly, proposed to Christine on her birthday (April 19), we would be married on my birthday, July 1.

Our marriage was consummated as planned, in Hawaii, where we still live today. It only happened because I had finally seen fit to make that ultimate commitment—one that had been difficult to make when I was married to Maria and then Shirlee. I went through quite a lot to reach the point I think I am at, as a person, today.

It's the same with the cookie business and being Famous Amos. I had to go through a lot in order to be the right person for that job. There was a whole process I went through, educating myself, and at the same time teaching people to do what I had learned. Anyone who believes that what happened to me came easy, or overnight, is terribly incorrect. The only things that happened overnight were sleepless nights, of which there were many. Most of all, my day-to-day, night-in-and-night-out concerns were about Famous Amos continuing until the next batch of money came in from somewhere, anywhere, and from anyone.

Also, I am constantly amazed and amused at how many people think I'm a millionaire; they see Famous Amos as being larger than it is. Well, that's what my promotions are all about —the entertainment, the fun—which I happily carry out as an employee of The Famous Amos Chocolate Chip Cookie Corporation. I'm an employee of Famous Amos, working for a salary, which, unbeknownst to many people, is the reason I started Famous Amos. I had to find some way to get off of that treadmill.

12

To give and to receive are one in truth.

I was not aware that with success and fame comes the fact that a major part of the population look up to you and might very well do anything you request. That, to me, was a tremendous amount of power, an extraordinary piece of influence I had never possessed or envisioned ever having. However, about the time I became cognizant of this privilege, I was also given some insight, paraphrased from the New Testament, as to what must be done with fame: "To whom much is given, much is expected."

That quotation told me what I had to do. I had arrived at the decision that being famous only means a lot of people know you. Promoting Famous Amos had certainly done that, but it had also made me aware that I needed to route my fame into other areas—areas in which I might be able to help others and, in essence, give back some of the fruits of my own success. It was time for me to do as a certain song says: "Reach out and touch somebody's hand. . . ."

Four years before I was Famous Amos—when I was Wally Amos, private citizen—I was compelled to "reach out and touch," because I was so touched by the effort, love, and humanity which were permeating a location in the southwest area of Los Angeles called St. Elmo Village. It was through a friend named Teddi Stewart that I came to know about St. Elmo Village, which was not really a village but a complex of small houses located in a heavily populated black community.

The reason we were there was to attend a fund raiser. Dinners were being sold for two dollars each to raise enough money for a deposit on the down payment needed to buy this property, to save it from becoming the site of an apartment building. Instead of becoming an apartment, what was once a "shoebox" was later turned into an enormous mural.

"Just because you live in a shoebox doesn't mean it has to look like a shoebox," was the explanation I received from Rozzell Sykes when I praised the colorful and creatively conceived location. It was Rozzell and his nephew Roderick, two artists, who had taken what could have been just another black ghetto neighborhood eyesore and, literally, transformed it into a work of art. What that metamorphosis entailed was replacing the old roofs of ten dilapidated houses, planting new shrubbery and trees, and applying bright paint, which they had to beg or borrow, to the interiors, exteriors, and driveways. St. Elmo Village also became a place where the community kids and adults could come and express themselves through art and community. With minimum instructions, the children were told that they could draw, sculpt, or paint, express themselves, and not be inhibited.

Looking around at St. Elmo Village, the works of art and this wonderful showcase, I could not hold back my enthusiasm for Rozzell's and Roderick's courage in taking on what seemed to be a monumental task. Rozzell, who is always eloquent and meticulous in his selection of words, said to me, "Whatever you have can always be better than it is. You *don't* have to settle for what it is, and it is up to each individual to make his place, or his life, the very best."

It was unfortunate that Rozzell's words and philosophy were felt only by the children at St. Elmo Village and by people like myself who could see and appreciate what he and his nephew had done. There was a spirit at St. Elmo which you could feel immediately, but I soon learned that it was not yet a community spirit. First of all, the owner of the location did not want to sell it to the Sykeses. And the people who lived on the street from which St. Elmo Village derived its name were not supportive of the project. That disturbed me. I had to do something, even though my funds were limited. I was committed to supporting St. Elmo Village and all it stood for.

The first thing I did was to seek out my friends in the entertainment community. Steve Allen eventually did a television show from St. Elmo; a local show on KNBC-TV called "The Sunday Show" originated one of their shows from the St. Elmo location; and my friend Sam Denoff, a prominent television writer-producer, and I had a joint birthday party there since our birthdays fall on the same date. Sam is slightly older, so to make him feel good I average our ages. Our request to the hundreds of guests we invited was that they give their gift to St. Elmo instead of Sam and me, so that St. Elmo would be assured of having its own happy birthday the following year. Doing these things was my way of trying to help St. Elmo raise the $15,000 needed as a down payment on the property, which they eventually did.

Some other things were also accomplished. For one, the mayor of Los Angeles, Thomas Bradley, showed his own support on behalf of the city of Los Angeles by establishing each Memorial Day as a day of celebration for St. Elmo Village. This, naturally, brought a great deal of media attention to St. Elmo and the community it is located in. So pretty soon the surrounding community got involved, and they too started to work to change their "shoebox" into something to be proud of.

Later, when I became Famous Amos, I was able to increase my support for St. Elmo Village, which I had told Rozzell and Roderick they could depend on. One of the first things I did was have the children of St. Elmo turn the parking lot of the Hollywood store into one large mural, thus helping my own "shoebox" look like something special; and St. Elmo Village received money for doing the work. I had always thought of the cookie store as an extension of St. Elmo Village. Other people decided they wanted bright-colored paint put in the right creative hands, so these same children from St. Elmo were asked to paint murals in other parts of Los Angeles. Once again it was confirmation that by helping others you help yourself.

I'm indebted to the Sykeses and St. Elmo Village for providing me a lesson in love and insight into what my own potential was. One thing I found, I did not need a lot of trimmings, or fancy stuff, to get by in life. All I needed were the bare necessities and an imagination, which can take a little and turn it into so much more. Those were the thoughts which drove me on when Famous Amos and the Hollywood store were in the formative and building stages. Even though I'm not able to visit or be around St. Elmo as much as I did in the past, because I live in Hawaii, the spirit of what St. Elmo Village represents is with me, as are the words of Rozzell Sykes, which are what St. Elmo Village is all about: "While everyone else is doing their worst, I will continue to do my best."

Rozzell Sykes's words were very much a part of the thinking of Dennis Martin, head librarian of Hollypark Library in Hawthorne, California, when he told me about his program of getting children to read and asked me if I would get involved with the program. The first meeting with the kids was during Black History Week, in 1977, when I gave out cookies and posters. The reaction to me was so enthusiastic that Dennis came up with the idea of a reading challenge for the kids, with the reward being Famous Amos Chocolate Chip Cookies. I liked the idea of my cookies being the "sweetener" to what many kids consider a bitter chore: improving their reading skills.

It was a three-month program at Hollypark Library, and every child who read eight books in a two-week period, plus wrote a report on the books they had read, received a one-pound bag of cookies as a reward. The minute the kids heard about the program, 520 of them signed up—the highest registration the library ever had. The program was also a success; Famous Amos gladly gave away 1,500 pounds of cookies to those readers who qualified. However, there was some bitterness about what my "sweeteners" were doing.

Word had gotten around that Dennis' program was a form of "bribing" the kids to read, which brought out the bureaucrats. They felt that rewarding kids with cookies did not help them to show incentive. When I heard that I thought how narrow-minded these people were not to see the good Dennis Martin was doing. What's wrong with bribing someone—anyone—

to enhance his or her life? If the end result is going to help the person being bribed, then do it: bribe him! That was my feeling, and it was eventually understood by the bureaucrats, and the program continued, with great success.

The Hollypark Library program turned out to be the beginning—actually the training ground—for what I would totally commit my time and fame to. One of the things the Hollypark program pointed out to me was that kids who did not read well often had parents who were not able to read. What a pity, I thought, especially if this was a broad problem. I was really feeling like doing something . . . something more. But I chose not to go the usual celebrity route of helping the physically handicapped—I felt that was well covered, and working. No, I wanted to find that other area of need, that something sitting right in front of us that needs attention.

Well, as Divine Order had willed it, my business associate, John Rosica, came to me one day to tell me about a friend of his who was a volunteer tutor for Literacy Volunteers of America. It was an organization I was not familiar with, and neither were most people in America. I also doubt that many people know there are over 23,000,000 native-born adult Americans who cannot read or write and are labeled "functional illiterates." That means they read at a fifth grade reading level or less. Shocking? You're right. You can imagine how I felt hearing this. I knew right away I wanted and *needed* to be with Literacy Volunteers of America.

Many people believed that I support LVA because I came from Florida and had problems reading at some point in time. Not so. I just felt the need to give something back. My mother and father could not read, but I never tied that in, or multiplied it by 23,000,000. I just felt they could not read because of the circumstances in which they lived, and because of segregation, which is true of a lot of blacks who cannot read and write today. However, the majority of the nonreaders are white, because the majority of the population is white.

Most of us take for granted that everybody can read because *we* can. That's because most of us live in little boxes with blinders on, and we're not concerned about the problems of other people. A person who cannot read or write is a person just barely existing. To that person, each day is a hopeless one, I'm sure. That's what I wanted to help LVA erase. I wanted to let the nonreaders know that "Today is God's gift to you. What you do with it is your gift to God." That being able to read simply meant acquiring the skill.

I went with John Rosica to LVA's headquarters in Syracuse, New York, to ask them if I could serve them as their national spokesperson. We met with the executive board and Ruth Colvin, who had founded the organization in 1962. At that time she wanted to help the many people who could not read and write in her Syracuse community. Later Mrs. Colvin expanded on her idea by working with professional reading consultants to develop a training method for nonprofessional volunteers to teach basic reading and writing to adults and teenagers. The method was successful, and LVA spread to other states and communities. There were, however, still a lot of places unaware of LVA, and I wanted to spread the word to those places.

Because the people of LVA are very reputable, they were naturally suspicious of me and my intentions. I made it clear to them I was not going to stop selling cookies during my promotions. But I would certainly be selling LVA also. I then told them of my belief that I could get people to understand what LVA could do for them; I could raise money, get new tutors, and work to give LVA much greater national exposure. I also committed myself to learning how LVA functioned so that as a spokesperson I could be truly representative.

In 1979 I was selected to be the National Spokesperson for LVA. As I had promised, I went to Syracuse and took an abbreviated training course for the program. April 10, 1979, I was officially introduced at a press conference, held at the Lincoln Center Library, as the National Spokesperson. From that day until now I have been working to make new friends for Literacy Volunteers of America, at my own expense. I'm pleased to say that by helping others I have been helped immensely.

One special moment occurred in November 1980, when the State Board of Education, the Adult Education Department, and LVA in the city of Franklin Township, New Jersey, decided to attack the problem of illiteracy and asked me to help bring attention to the program. I was also asked to participate in the dedication ceremony of the town's new library. However, that was only the beginning of what I would be doing. Actually, a great job had been done in rallying the entire community to participate in the program. So I was there to reach those who had not already been made aware of the program. When I arrived, on November 21, "Famous Amos Day" was declared—I did my usual thing as Famous Amos, and then I participated in a ceremony at which awards were presented to people in LVA programs. I was also to be the guest speaker at a rally at Franklin High School, which was an honor. I doubted, though, that there would be a big turnout since this was the night the person who shot "J. R. Ewing," on the popular television series "Dallas," would be revealed.

Well, I misread the people of Franklin Township, who obviously were not as interested in J.R.'s assailant as they were in hearing what Famous Amos had to say. The auditorium was filled to capacity, and my speech was well received. Then I was given a surprise; a high school diploma was presented to me from Franklin High School. It was one of the few times in my life that I was speechless. I was flabbergasted! Somehow it was discovered that I had not graduated officially from high school, so Franklin High School decided to correct that. They also filled my heart with happiness. The best was yet to come, however, because I would see LVA at work and see it help someone I knew personally.

Shortly after I was kindly cited as being educated, I went home to Tallahassee to renew my education as far as my roots were concerned. Somehow over the years I had tried to erase my memory of where I came from, but once I got back home I realized I had been wrong. Your roots are important; they're your heritage—good or bad—and your life, and are responsible in many ways for making you the way you are. Well, for the short while I was in Tallahassee I learned a lot of things about the way I was. But I also found out about some other people, one person in particular named Jaycee Oliver.

Jaycee was married to a former neighbor of mine named
Marie Robinson, and they lived on an acre of land in a very
comfortable home. During my visit Christine and I were invited for dinner, during which we renewed old memories with
Marie and met her husband. Jaycee was a big guy around forty-
four years old, a large body of joy and happiness, and a positive
thinker—something I particularly liked about him. When this
pleasurable evening came to a close, I showed my appreciation
by giving them a tin of The Famous Amos Chocolate Chip
Cookies.

When I returned home to Hawaii, Jaycee called me to ask
about getting some more cookies in the tin, since they had
shared theirs with friends and were willing to buy more. I explained the procedure for ordering, but realized that what Jaycee had done was collect enough money for twenty to twenty-
five tins of cookies. I warned him that he might be putting too
much time into getting cookies for his friends. Jaycee said he
didn't mind, because that was his way of trying to increase sales
of Famous Amos cookies in his area. I liked his good intentions, so I explained to him how he could buy wholesale from
Famous Amos, which we paid the freight for, and sell them to
his friends at retail. Jaycee took my advice, and before long he
was up to twenty to twenty-five cases. He also, with those kinds
of sales, became the Famous Amos distributor in Tallahassee.
Jaycee was amazed, but he also wanted to do more—more than
he could do without more money. Well, Jaycee had too much
ambition and drive, plus he worked too hard, for me not to
loan him the money to get his operation going, so I did.

Jaycee then went into business as a part-time Famous
Amos distributor. He handled his distribution during his lunch
hour and after working his regular job, which was for a car
dealer. Jaycee had been with them twenty-three years but only
made four dollars an hour. He had no insurance or hospi-
talization and no pension. His salary was all he had, and for a
special reason: my newly found entrepreneur could not read or
write.

Although Jaycee used common sense, a strong initiative,
which was strengthened by his desire to do something for him-

self, he needed what LVA's program had to offer. So I explained to him that he would have to be able to read and write if he wanted his operation to grow. Jaycee didn't go down to defeat; he immediately asked how he could get started with LVA. That was easy, because LVA had recently started offering programs in Tallahassee. In no time Jaycee was working with a tutor, plus listening to his lessons on cassette, which enabled him to study while driving his truck and delivering cookies.

Jaycee not only excelled in his own program, he became a spokesman for LVA. This was particularly good because LVA needs students in the program to go out and talk to other nonreaders and let them know about LVA and how they can be helped. This is important because people who can't read are shy about coming forth and admitting it. They feel, thanks to our society, as though they're looked down on. That's why nonreaders are essential in getting other nonreaders to accept the help available at LVA. When Jaycee understood this, he not only became a top Famous Amos distributor, he left very few nonreader doors unknocked on.

The proof that Jaycee had been helped by LVA came when he decided to give up his job with the car dealership to devote all his energy to distributing Famous Amos cookies. Jaycee, for me, epitomizes the words of Karen Ravin when she wrote, "To achieve all that is possible, we must attempt the impossible. To be as much as we can be, we must dream of being more."

For many reasons Jaycee's association with Famous Amos did not continue. However, the mere fact that he had the opportunity to run his own business will have a lasting positive effect on his life. I know it will on mine. Also, Jaycee's involvement with LVA gives real meaning to the quote "As I walked down the path of life I didn't leave a footprint until I learned to read."

My own experience with LVA has been priceless, and I feel a special indebtedness to them for giving me the opportunity to serve them. It has made me feel useful to a community that needs me, needs the help I can offer because I'm a celebrity. For that reason, I feel very fortunate. I was equally fortunate to receive an invitation to become a member of the Board of Directors of the Friends of Libraries, U.S.A., which gives me the opportunity to increase my commitment to doing something further about the problems of nonreaders and promoting the use of our nation's libraries.

Reaching out and touching those who need your help is certainly gratifying, and good for the soul. That's what fame did for me. On the lighter side, it also brought me into contact with more people named Amos than I had ever known existed!

I am convinced there is more to life than meets the eye. If not, then why would my path eventually be crossed by yet another *Amos* named John? I am also certain that my decision to remove the hatred I had for the *former* John Amos made it possible for me to accept the *new* John Amos in my life, even to the point of letting him, literally, get into the mouth that feeds me.

As Famous Amos I have probably become as famous for my broad smiles as I have for my crazy promotional antics and my chocolate chip cookies. But none of that might have been retained had I not met this Amos named John, a dentist, located in San Francisco.

I met John during a promotion at Macy's Cellar in San Francisco. During my get-acquainted fun and frolics, a young woman named Marie asked me, as so many people did, to autograph a bag of cookies for her boss. I asked her what she did, and learned that she was an assistant to her boss, who was a dentist. She also said his name was Amos. Well, I just had to say hello to somebody named *Amos*, so I autographed the bag of cookies and Marie left.

Not too long after, I was approached by a man who must have been about 5'6" tall, and who seemed to be a cross between Dustin Hoffman and Clint Eastwood. I offered him a cookie, which is one of my ways of making friends, both for myself and for the cookie. Before he took the cookie he asked me if they had nuts, which they did. He then said, "I'm allergic to nuts, and even if I could eat them I wouldn't take a cookie from you because you're an impostor."

I was floored. But, after studying my assailant, and discovering the very cleverly disguised sense of humor of this man, I collected myself, and in typical Famous Amos craziness, I yelled out, "It must be Amos the dentist!" A smile crossed his face, and I knew I was right. Then I started letting everyone know "Here is the real Famous Amos!" I liked John the dentist immediately. His soft-spoken, laid-back, and personable way made me feel very comfortable, and I knew that I had met an Amos I was proud to make a friend.

Now, for anyone who has ever wondered about my toothpaste smile, and how it's remained so perfect, wonder no longer. I wear dentures, and I have been wearing them since I was twenty-four years old. I had been wearing my present set of dentures about fourteen years, and they were worn to almost nothing. I had known for a long time that I should get new ones, but I never took the time to find a dentist to do the work. But, now, I had the opportunity to act. I couldn't take the chance of my dentures falling out again at Bill Cosby's feet while I laughed at one of his jokes, as my uppers had done once before.

Therefore, John was hired to provide me with a new smile. After several trips to San Francisco, my new dentures were ready for me to wear and the world to see. John was proud and pleased with his work, as was I, since it allowed me to "keep the business in the Amos family." Shortly after that I was able to make John Amos, the dentist, truly a "famous" Amos when I displayed the smile he gave me on the cover of the June 1977 issue of *Time*.

Although being Famous Amos did bring in a larger crop of friends, and many named Amos, I must admit I was taken by surprise when I met an Amos from "down under," Australia.

In fact, I met this Australian Amos, named Ken, at a time when Famous Amos was, I thought, not that famous. Because we were still growing legs, as they say, and developing friends, we were ourselves down under as a business. But that never interfered with my desire, and need, I suppose, to always project a happy image, especially to strangers. So, when this Australian tour group bus stopped in front of the Hollywood store, I did as I always would do with American tourists: I boarded the bus with balloons and cookies, which I passed out while I was being my old happy-go-lucky self. This time, however, with the Australians, I found out just how famous Famous Amos really was, and I also met another Amos who will always be "famous" to me.

Ken Amos, who is from North Ryde, New South Wales, Australia, was part of this tour group visiting Hollywood and Beverly Hills. They were on one of those tours which points out where the stars live, and they had requested that they get to visit my Famous Amos store in Hollywood. That happened because of a commercial I had done for Qantas Airways which was shown throughout Australia. So, that meant Famous Amos was already quite famous down under. That was a relief, because I was fearful my Australian tourist friends had come to picket me for daring to call a "biscuit" a cookie. Whether that was ever on their minds, I never found out. But I did try to find out something about these new friends, starting with their names. Suddenly, a voice said, "Ken Amos." Well, hearing "Amos," and with an Australian accent, was something by itself. But realizing that even in Australia I had a kinship was astounding to me. I grabbed Ken's hand and began shaking it vigorously, at the same time proclaiming to everyone that Ken Amos was really my long-lost brother. This, of course, received a great deal of laughter, because Ken Amos was as white as I am black.

But despite all my clowning, and having a great time with our Australian visitors, I suddenly realized something. Here was Ken, whose skin color was different than mine, and whose home was approximately nine thousand miles away on the other side of the world, but who was truly as excited at meeting me as I was at meeting him. I also felt that maybe he was thinking what I was thinking; that possibly there was a kinship between us that neither of us knew about. At any rate, I decided I would insure that Ken Amos never forgot me. I loaded him down with Famous Amos memorabilia and anything I thought would help to solidify as well as show my happiness at meeting someone I really did feel was a "brother."

Some time later, while on a promotional tour for Famous Amos in Sydney, I got to see my Australian brother again. Ken had heard I was coming to town. So, he came to Sydney to welcome me. When I saw him, I embraced him with an affection that one has for a brother, once again proudly proclaiming our kinship, much to his surprise. But I got the feeling that this shy man was happy to also be able to say that his brother was a Yank named Famous Amos.

Historically speaking, it was ironic that I should be in Washington, D.C., on November 18, 1980, only two weeks after one of my former show business colleagues, Ronald Reagan, had been elected by the people to be the fortieth President of the United States. My own reason for being in the nation's capital was just as auspicious: I had been selected by the Smithsonian Institution of the National Museum of American History to become a part of the exhibits in the Business Americana collection. Such an offer was nonpareil for a number of reasons, the most important being that I, Famous Amos, would now become a part of the history of the country of my birth.

Becoming a page in your country's history is not easy. For sure, it was not one of the goals I set for myself as a youth while growing to manhood in Tallahassee, Florida, and in New York City. Nor was it something I saw happening to me when I worked as a clerk at Saks Fifth Avenue, or when I went into show business. I always tried to do what I could to make my clients as well known as possible, but that did not include me. I never thought I wanted to be famous.

But the work of God is something none of us can question. To me, one of the most meaningful sentences in the Lord's Prayer is, "Thy will be done." Divine Order will choose the time, but prior to all of that we do a great deal of work in order to reach the pinnacle of success, whatever that is or will be. Therefore that part of the work which consumed a lot of time, a lot of devotion, a lot of hard work, and a great deal of love was not carried on by myself alone. I was fortunate in that I met people who were willing to share my dream. True, it was *my* dream initially. But it was their volumes upon volumes of work that went into the so-called "rough draft" which eventually became that page in American history with *my* name on it. So it's important to me to put into perspective just how I got to the Smithsonian Institution, and who was responsible, or my being there would be for naught.

The only thoughts I had about history when I started Famous Amos was my attempt to find a history of the chocolate chip cookie. I had, during the time I was putting everything together, a need to know just how it all began. I not only felt I wanted to know, but everyone was entitled to know the origin of this tasty morsel. I wanted to know the creative person, and mind, who saw fit to bring so much passion to our taste buds. But, with all my seeking, searching, and asking, I could never find any answers.

Therefore it was necessary for me to create my own history; or, more precisely, Chuck Casell created a history for me. What I had given Chuck to work with were the results of my many trips to the Los Angeles Main Public Library, where I went through book after book and found nothing but recipes, and no mention of Ruth Wakefield, whom I would learn about later. During that search I had come in contact with the years 1929 and 1939 as possible birth dates of the cookie, but I didn't know which was correct. I did know that Massachusetts was the state where "something" had happened with chocolate chip cookies. I also knew that a history was as important to the outside of the bag as the cookies were to the inside. So Chuck became the victim of my daily yearnings for "a brief history," and I never let up. Neither did Chuck Casell. Then, one day, he had it; Chuck had found the right thought, the right words, and they were as follows:

1929 was a bad year for most things. But it was a good year for the chocolate chip cookie.

It was then, in a tiny farmhouse kitchen in Lowell, Massachusetts, that the first chocolate chip cookie was baked. In fact, that day has come to be known as Brown

Thursday. (Not to be confused with Black Tuesday or Blue Monday.)

Over the years, millions have slaved over hot stoves trying to recapture the sensational taste created on that glorious day in Lowell. But not until 1970, when Wally Amos started to bake his secret recipe, has any chocolate chip cookie been so thoroughly authentic and delicious at the same time. So enjoy these "Famous Amos" chocolate chip cookies and have a very brown day.

From my research, I knew there was a city called Lowell. So, when Chuck requested a city to go with the state of Massachusetts, I chose Lowell because I had worked with a client named Lowell Fulsom, who is a great blues singer. The two Lowells just popped into my mind. As for the year 1929, that was simply the best of two choices, and Chuck, being the fine writer he was, took poetic license, just as I had decided to take historical license to give the chocolate chip cookie a history.

It was a fun thing, a fun trip I had taken with the words Chuck and I agreed upon for the history. It was a comedy with no willful desire to take credit for something I knew I had not created. Hell, as far as I was concerned, and for as many years as I could remember, it was my Aunt Della who was the creator of chocolate chip cookies. My Aunt Della's chocolate chip cookies were the only ones I knew, the only ones I was willing to eat. However, history, as I learned later, when tampered with, will turn around and tell you you're wrong—especially if you make history yourself.

A little over a year after Famous Amos cookies were well known from coast to coast, a writer named Arthur Lubow wrote in an article for *New Times* magazine that my history was categorically incorrect. He wrote in his article: ". . . in the beautiful Massachusetts seaside town of Duxbury, at the end of a country lane, overlooking the ocean and a private dock, there stands a green and brown mansion surrounded by trees . . ." which turned out to be the location where Ruth Wakefield, a gray-haired lady in her seventies, lived. She was the creator of the chocolate chip cookie, and as Lubow also

pointed out, Mrs. Wakefield and her husband had run the Toll
House Inn in Whitman, Massachusetts, for forty years. It was
in the early 1930s that Mrs. Wakefield created the chocolate
chip cookie and named it after her restaurant.

If Arthur Lubow had been close to me when I read his
article, I would have hugged him for having set the record
straight. I did not agree, however, that his article implied that I
had purposely created a historical gambit for my own benefit.
That was not true; I just had not known, just as Lubow did not
know that Mrs. Wakefield had actually called her creations
"Toll House Chocolate *Crunch* Cookies." I discovered that
fact in a book entitled *Ruth Wakefield's Toll House Tried and
True Recipes*, which was first published in 1936. I had received
this book from a Mrs. Albert Martin, who lived in Warwick,
Rhode Island, after she had heard me mention Mrs. Wakefield
on the Larry King Mutual network radio talk show.

The article by Lubow actually helped me take my first
steps toward meeting Ruth Wakefield. First I tried to contact
her by telephone in Duxbury, Massachusetts, but the operator
said there were three Ruth Wakefields listed. Then, after I
talked with the long-distance operator and let her know I was
Famous Amos, she became as excited as I was and worked
diligently to get me the correct telephone number. This was
like going to Mecca for me, going to the source. Then the operator did get the correct number, and it was as if I had found
gold. But for some reason I never made the call. For some
reason or another, which is not clear to me, I kept putting off
the call; a bit of procrastination on my part which I still regret.

In January 1977 I read a newspaper article which said
Ruth Wakefield had passed away. I was disappointed, to say
the least, not to have talked with her. It would have been such
a pleasure to be able to tell her how much I loved her, and how
thankful I and millions of others were for the contribution she
had made to the world. She had created history, although she
remained, for the most part, in obscurity.

Actually, it was the Nestlé's Company that brought Mrs.
Wakefield to the public's attention, and she was responsible for
showing Nestlé's how to make better use of their semi-sweet

chocolate bar. She was also the reason Nestlé's had an increase
in sales of their chocolate bar. Mrs. Wakefield was using it in
her first attempts at creating what would eventually be called
chocolate chip cookies, but which she named Toll House Chocolate Crunch Cookies. Back then the chocolate did not melt
while the cookies were baking. After they cooled, they retained
their crunchiness, so that when you bit down on the cookies
you could actually hear a "crunch" sound.

In those days, around 1938, chocolate chip morsels were
not available, and the distributor did not have Baker's Chocolate in stock. So Mrs. Wakefield used Nestlé's semi-sweet bars,
which she would cut into little chunks to put into her cookies.
The chocolate she had been using was about to be discontinued; then Nestlé's saw a sudden increase in sales in the New
England area. They investigated and found out the reason was
Ruth Wakefield's baking of chocolate cookies. Nestlé's bought
all rights to her cookies, and the recipe for her Toll House
Chocolate Cookies was put on the backs of the packages of
chocolate bars so people could bake their own cookies at home.
Later the same recipe was placed on the backs of their packages
of morsels. Mrs. Wakefield also became a consultant for
Nestlé's.

Lowell, Massachusetts, was real, although not the Mecca
for chocolate chip cookies. It was really a mill city, so the "tiny
farmhouse kitchen in Lowell" I spoke of in my history would
never have existed. Had it existed, it would have stood out like
a sore thumb in this quaint New England town, which was actually the birthplace of the Industrial Revolution. After I was
suitably apprised of Mrs. Wakefield's location, I was invited to
visit Lowell, where I admitted to the people there that what I
had done was a put-on. The kind people of Lowell did not hold
it against me. They, in fact, appreciated my bringing their city
to the attention of the millions of people who were buying Famous Amos cookies. I even became friends with two of Lowell's distinguished citizens, U.S. Senator Paul Tsongas and Jerry
Dunfey of the Dunfey hotel chain. So, even with the falsehood,
some redeeming good was accomplished; Lowell became well

known, and I made a whole new city of friends for Famous
Amos cookies.

It became obvious to me, as I saw Famous Amos spreading, that I had become more famous than I had anticipated.
Even some of my closest friends could not believe that "a simple chocolate chip cookie" created all the attention I had received. I had become, as they say, "as American as apple pie,"
except that I had done it with chocolate chip cookies. So I was
really as "American as chocolate chip cookies." It was just that
kind of thinking which was going through my mind when I
read a newspaper that ignited my curiosity. The Smithsonian
Institution had decided to accept the leather jacket of the
Fonz, from the television series, "Happy Days," as a part of
their collection to be exhibited. The jacket was being selected
because it was a permanent part of American history. Hell, I
thought, Famous Amos is a part of American history too! A
very real part, whereas the Fonz was a fictional part. Therefore
I decided that if the Smithsonian would accept the jacket off of
the Fonz's back they should be willing to accept the shirt and
the hat that have become identified with America, and most assuredly with its business history, off of my back, and the hat off
of my head, as well.

So I told my public relations representatives, John and
Marilyn Rosica, "Let's go fishing," and they agreed. That, by
the way, is our way of saying that we'll go out and see what we
can get, and if we don't get anything, then we haven't lost anything either. Our "fishing expedition" began with a letter to
the Smithsonian, which was answered with "maybe" and "we'll
see." We followed with another letter and some publicity materials, as well as the suggestion of having a meeting, which they
agreed to. Marilyn and John went to Washington, D.C., and
met with the curator, Dr. John Hoffman, and laid out for
him how they felt my inclusion could be accomplished. Dr.
Hoffman said they would weigh the suggestions and get back to
us. From the time we started in February 1980, with several
pieces of correspondence, and additional meetings to reiterate
what we had already said, we never thought it would not hap-

pen. We also maintained our tenacity. It eventually paid off with Famous Amos being selected for the Smithsonian Institution at the National Museum of American History.

It was decided that the shirt and the hat I'm wearing in the photograph that appears on the bag of my cookies would be placed on exhibit in the Business Americana collection. It also meant that Famous Amos would be the first food company to have anything accepted at the Smithsonian. Also I would be the first black businessman ever to have anything accepted in that collection.

Prior to my installation on November 18, 1980, there were several pieces of correspondence, including the shipment of the articles to be placed on exhibit. This, of course, resulted in moments of nostalgia for me. I remembered how I had acquired the panama hat, which took me back to Florence, Alabama, a city across the river from Muscle Shoals. My client, Mississippi Charles Bevel, was recording an album in Muscle Shoals. It was in Florence that I purchased the hat for ten dollars, which was cheap since similar panamas usually cost thirty dollars or more. It was a bargain, but the hat was a tight fit, and I didn't like the band on it. But I did want the hat, so I decided I would get a haircut to let the hat fit my head, and I would simply use the band of another panama hat I already had which was ready for retirement. The original hat that I sent to the Smithsonian from Hawaii was old from wearing. When Dr. Hoffman received it, he questioned whether it was the right hat. I informed the good doctor, "That's it! You've got the one and only original panama hat, including all the sweat stains and aging."

As for the shirt on my back—the Indian-style gauze shirt I'm wearing in the photograph—that was purchased in New York's Greenwich Village around 1973. This was during my change from Beverly Hills to Hollywood, an economical change and a style change as well. I bought those kinds of shirts because my money had reached an all-time low. Wash and wear was also the cheapest way to go. However, that wash-and-wear shirt became world renowned and was now going to be a part of American history.

At the time I started wearing those clothes, being in the cookie business and one day being on display at the Smithsonian never entered my mind. The fact that I had never been to the Smithsonian Institution might have had something to do with that. So, on the day of my installation, I was amazed when I saw what was there; for instance, Charles Lindbergh's plane, the *Spirit of St. Louis*, which made me think, "My God, here I am in the same building with *that!*" Chills ran up my spine, along with tears in my heart, which was how I felt at the moment. But the biggest thrill was when I saw my own display: the hat, the shirt, and the bag and tin of cookies, all sitting on a mahogany table with some dried flowers embellishing them. They *really* looked like they belonged in the museum. I became emotional—choked up—and I fought to hold back the tears.

Then I entered the reception room, with Christine at my side, and I met a large turnout of dignitaries and representatives of the media—*Time*, the Washington *Post*, NBC-TV, the Voice of America—as well as friends and well-wishers, all watching my trip to the podium. After I was officially received in the Smithsonian Institution, I said a few words about what a great experience it was for me. I explained to everyone present what becoming a part of American history meant to me, someone who was not even a high school graduate. I also said that this was a moment of revelation, that it was the free enterprise system in our country which had made it possible for me to achieve what I had.

> "You can do whatever you want to do.
> I didn't even graduate from high school,
> but I tried really hard to make it,
> despite that setback. Determination is
> all it takes. . . ."

Those were not just made-up words, or a speech. I sincerely believe that to be true for *anyone*. I also believe that if it could happen to me, Wally Amos, who went on to become better known as Famous Amos, then it can happen to *you*.

EPILOGUE

Writing this book has been a tremendous learning experience for me. It has given me the opportunity to really get to know myself better. I have also purged myself of many of the negative feelings I had been holding on to and I have forgiven myself for many of my past mistakes. I have no doubt that writing the book has given me a firmer hold on today and a happier tomorrow.

I truly feel that my success is merely another example that it is possible to achieve and be successful on whatever level you desire. Actually, that can be said of anyone's success, for in reality we are all teachers and we are all students. It is my hope that you get the one message that I feel my accomplishments convey. That message is simply, "If he can do it, so can I."

We began the book with a positive message and I would like to leave you with a positive message. It deals with determination, perseverance, and an undying belief in yourself. Those have to be three of the main ingredients that enabled me to get Famous Amos started and then to keep it going. There were many times when people told me I would never be able to do it. But I just held to the thought, "I can, I can, I can" and sure enough I did. So, thanks for reading the book and always remember the following poem, "It Couldn't Be Done," by Edgar A. Guest.

> Somebody said that it couldn't be done
> But he with a chuckle replied
> That maybe it couldn't, but he would be one
> Who wouldn't say so till he'd tried
> So he buckled right in with the trace of a grin

On his face. If he worried he hid it.
He started to sing as he tackled the thing
That couldn't be done, and he did it.

Somebody scoffed: "Oh, you'll never do that;
At least no one has ever done it."
But he took off his coat and he took off his hat,
And the first thing we knew he'd begun it.
With a lift of his chin and a bit of a grin
Without any doubting or quiddit
He started to sing as he tackled the thing
That couldn't be done, and he did it.

There are thousands to tell you it cannot be done,
There are thousands to prophesy failure
There are thousands to point out to you, one by one,
The dangers that wait to assail you.
But just buckle right in with a bit of a grin.
Just take off your coat and go to it;
Just start to sing as you tackle the thing
That "cannot be done," and you'll do it.

Aloha,
Wally

The Famous Amos Handy Guide to Making Very Brown Chocolate Chip Cookies

1. Take whatever chocolate chip cookie recipe you have been using and follow it very closely. A tip: use any member of the nut family you wish; raisins or figs are also good. Another tip: cookies made with margarine taste just as good as those made with butter, although they tend to talk back.

2. If you have been mixing your cookies manually in a bowl with a wooden spoon, as I did for five years, you may consider purchasing an electric mixer; although a Cuisinart serves many purposes in the kitchen, it does not mix cookie dough well, because it chops the chips and nuts into teenie tiny pieces.

3. If you have cookie sheets that must be greased before using, the wrappers from the sticks of margarine or butter will do the job nicely.

4. Will Rogers said, "I never met a man I didn't like." Well, I never met an oven that bakes evenly, even the commercial ovens I use in my retail stores. If you want evenly brown, beautiful cookies, you must watch them closely and turn the cookie sheets several times during baking. This is also a good time to talk to your cookies. Tell them you love them, and that it's important for them to get as brown on the bottom as they are on the top. Let them know that they are about to bring a lot of joy and pleasure to people. Turning and talking works every time for me, and I bet it will for you too.

5. As for the proper baking temperature and time, 350 to 375 degrees seems to work well in most ovens. If you have an electric oven, try to keep your trays in the center of the oven. If they're too close to the top or bottom, one side of the cookies will burn. The time of baking is determined by whether you want a soft or a crisp cookie. Just remember that the longer you bake them, the crispier they become, no matter how much you talk to them.

6. Finally, the most important thing to remember when making chocolate chip cookies are the chips. So don't forget those semi-sweet chips, and *have a very brown day!*

The Famous Amos Guide to Things That Go Well with Chocolate Chip Cookies

We are all aware of the obvious things that people eat and drink with chocolate chip cookies: ice cream and milk. What I shall attempt to do is give you some suggestions that you might never think of, or may be too timid to consider.

One of my early discoveries was chocolate chip cookies with yogurt. Blackberry yogurt was my favorite. You get best results when you submerge the cookie in the yogurt and then scoop it out with a spoon. It is truly a taste treat par excellence.

Fruit being one of my favorite foods, I just had to come up with a way of eating chocolate chip cookies with fruit. Since I could not settle on one fruit, being fond of them all, I decided to cover about a half dozen cookies with a fruit salad. I allowed it to sit in the refrigerator for about ten minutes so that some of the fruit juice could penetrate the cookies. It is then ready to be eaten. It was indeed one of the most entertaining dishes I have ever passed through my mouth.

Then there was the time my wife, Christine, made cheese cake with chocolate chip cookie crumbs for the crust, which in itself is not so unusual. But when she mixed in large broken cookie pieces and served it with a thick chocolate sauce, it made my eyeballs spin.

There are numerous drinks that go well with chocolate chip cookies. At the top of my list is an ice cold fruit smoothie. I've also found that all fruit juices compliment chocolate chip cookies. As you know I have given "The Cookie" a few parties and the consensus is that champagne is by far the favorite beverage at a chocolate chip cookie party. If you're stuck for a drink you can't go wrong with plain old H$_2$O.

Those are just a few of my favorite things to eat or mix chocolate chip cookies with. I'm sure you also have your favorites. If you don't, I challenge you to be creatively daring and make some up.

During my eight years as a cookie person, there have been only two things that I've found absolutely did not go well with chocolate chip cookies. One was beer and the other was sashimi (raw fish). However, beer and sashimi go very well together. Happy cookie eating whatever side dish you choose.